Bariatric Cookbook Bible

The Most Complete and Step-By-Step Guide with 365 Days of Healthy Recipes with Up to 5 Ingredients to Cook in 30 Minutes or Less Specifically Designed for Gastric Sleeve Surgery. Meal and Physical Exercise Plans Included.

By

Alex Mc Corner

Contents

Introduction

When it comes to creating a healthy lifestyle, bariatric surgery is a big step to take, and it should not be taken lightly. These surgeries are typically the last option a doctor will offer to a patient, but they are extremely effective methods of losing weight when other methods have failed.

While the decision to have this type of surgery is between you and your doctor, it is beneficial to be prepared before the procedure. Knowing what you can and cannot cook will help to alleviate some of the stress.

You will be put on a low-carb, high-protein diet in the weeks leading up to your surgery to help shrink the size of your liver. You will be on a liquid diet for two days prior to surgery. Following surgery, you will undergo four distinct step-down eating phases, ranging from liquid to solid foods. But that doesn't mean you can't have fun with what you eat.

This book is here to help alleviate some of the stress associated with this process. There are hundreds of different recipes that you can enjoy at various stages of your healing process. There will be various liquids to enjoy during your first week following surgery, as well as recipes to enjoy for the rest of your life.

The best part is that you can have these before your surgery, at least before you start the liquid diet. Just because your food options are limited does not mean you have to sacrifice flavor. Many of these recipes are high in protein, which will keep you fuller for longer. You'll also find the serving size, so you'll know how many people you can share it with and how much you should eat.

Just a reminder that this book is not intended to be medical advice. This book is strictly for educational purposes. Only your physician can advise you on bariatric surgery. Regardless of what this book says, always follow the advice and rules that your surgeon and doctor give you before and after surgery.

There are many books on this subject available, thank you for selecting this one! Every effort has been made to include as much useful information as possible, so let's get started!

Chapter 1: Introduction of Bariatric Surgery

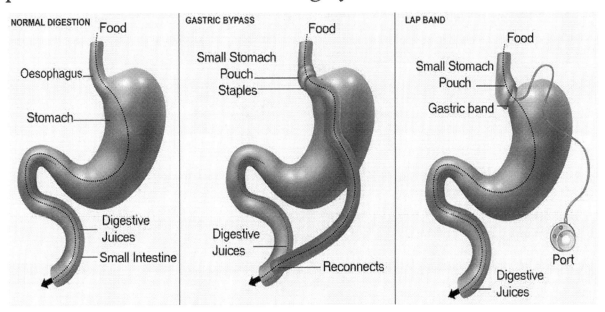

Weight loss surgery that works by altering the digestive system is known as bariatric surgery. There are a variety of weight loss surgeries that fall under the umbrella term "bariatric surgery," including gastric bypass.

Treating extreme obesity with just diet and exercise is usually unsuccessful. Assisting such people in their weight loss efforts is the goal of bariatric surgery. If patients with severe fatness also make changes to their diet and way of life after bariatric surgery, there is hope that their mortality rates can be lowered.

Bariatric surgery aims to reduce a patient's appetite while simultaneously decreasing their stomach and intestinal capacity to absorb nutrients.

Digestion begins in the mouth when food is chewed and combines with saliva and other secretions that contain enzymes. When the food reaches the stomach, digestive juices begin to break it down so that the body can absorb the nutrients and calories it contains. Digestion speeds up as liquid reaches the duodenum (the first section of the small intestine) and mixes with bile and pancreatic juice.

This natural process of breaking down and absorbing food is one that bariatric surgery aims to alter or disrupt. Patients can lose weight and protect themselves from obesity-related health problems by absorbing fewer nutrients and fewer calories.

1.1 Different Types of Bariatric Procedures and their Pros and Cons

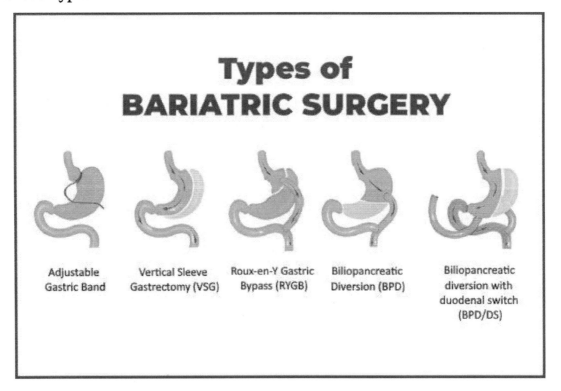

Choosing the most appropriate surgical option for weight loss among the many currently available can be challenging. This short overview of the various surgical methods for reducing excess weight can serve as a springboard for discussion with your doctor.

Right now, there are three major bariatric (weight loss) procedures being conducted in the US. Roux-en-Y gastric bypass, sleeve gastrectomy and Adjustable gastric banding are the three methods. None of these methods for losing weight is without risk or complications, and none of them is a quick fix. Surgery is only a tool to help you lose weight, and you still need to exercise and eat healthily to see results.

Those who have a body mass index (BMI) of 40 or higher, or a BMI of 35 or higher with co-morbid conditions, like high blood pressure or diabetes, may be candidates for weight loss surgery.

The Roux-en-Y gastric bypass (RYGB), laparoscopic sleeve gastrectomy (LSG), and adjustable gastric band are the most common bariatric surgeries today (AGB). All bariatric surgeries are designed to reduce hunger and promote portion control. Some surgeries, however, work at an even deeper metabolic level. Some surgeries have been shown to improve type 2 diabetes, hypertension, sleep apnea, fatty liver, and other comorbidities.

The expertise of your surgeon and medical team will be required to determine which procedure is best for you. Each surgery has advantages and disadvantages, but they all assist you in gaining control of your health. Whatever surgery you choose; you can be confident that it was the best decision for you.

1.1.1 The Roux-EN-Y Gastric Bypass

This procedure, also known as gastric bypass, is regarded as the "gold standard" of weight-loss surgery. The procedure is divided into two stages: First, your surgical team will divide the small intestine and create a small stomach pouch about one ounce in size. The pouch is then joined to the lower portion of the small intestine. When we eat, our food skips over the bulk of the stomach and the first part of the small intestine on its way from the stomach bag to the lower part of the intestine.

Pros

- Reduces stomach capacity and food intake

- Changes gut hormones in a positive way, reducing appetite and increasing satiety.

- Changes in energy expenditure that may aid in weight loss and maintenance

- If necessary, reversible.

- The likelihood of significant (60 to 80 percent) long-term excess weight loss with more than 50 percent maintenance

Cons

- Complication rates for gastric sleeve and band procedures are higher.

- Long-term vitamin and mineral deficiencies are high risk.

- Hospital stays that are the longest.

- Food intolerances and dumping syndrome are very likely.

1.1.2 Laparoscopic Sleeve Gastrectomy

Under the supervision of their surgical teams, sleeve patients will have approximately 80% of their stomachs removed. The procedure works by severely limiting the quantity of food the stomach can hold at one time, leaving only a small, tubular pouch the size of a banana. However, it has the greatest impact on gut hormones, which influence hunger, satiety, and blood sugar control.

Pros

- Reduces stomach capacity and food intake

- Changes gut hormones in a positive way, reducing appetite and increasing satiety.

- Compared to gastric bypass, there are fewer surgical complications.

- When compared to gastric bypass, there is a lower risk of dumping syndrome.

- It does not necessitate the use of a foreign device (as in a gastric band) or the rerouting of the food stream (as in gastric bypass)

- Shorter hospital stays in comparison to gastric bypass

- Possibility of significant (more than 50%) excess weight loss

Cons

- Long-term vitamin and mineral deficiencies are a possibility.

- The possibility of acid reflux

- Nonreversible

1.1.3 The Adjustable Gastric Band

An inflatable band is placed near the top of the stomach to create a small stomach pouch in gastric band procedures. Filling the band with saline through a port beneath the abdominal wall can gradually reduce the size of the pouch over time. The ease with which food moves from the small pouch into the lower stomach is affected by tightening the band in this manner. The pouch is intended to curb hunger and promote a sense of fullness.

Pros

- Reduces stomach capacity and restricts food consumption

- With no incisions in the stomach wall or intestines, the device is completely adjustable and reversible.

- Lowest rates of early post-operative surgical complications

- The least likely to suffer from vitamin and mineral deficiencies.

- Hospital stays that are the shortest.

- Excess weight loss of 40 to 50% is achieved.

Cons

- Weight loss is slower and less drastic than with gastric bypass and band procedures.

- It is necessary for a foreign device to remain in the body.

- Complications such as band slippage and erosion are possible.

- Overeating patients are at risk of esophageal dilation.

- The possibility of developing food intolerances to specific textures

- More frequent follow-ups are required for band adjustment.

- Highest re-operation rate

1.1.4 Biliopancreatic Diversion with the Duodenal Switch (BPD/DS)

Before the biliopancreatic diversion with the duodenal switch surgery or BPD-DS, a stomach pouch forms. This pouch looks like a tube and is the start of a sleeve gastrectomy. It is almost similar to the gastric bypass because more of the small intestine is bypassed. Since their stomachs are in the shape of bananas, they can eat less. The meal goes around about 75% of the small intestine. This is the most of any regularly used legal procedure. This makes it much harder for the body to absorb calories and nutrients. Patients must take mineral and vitamin supplements after surgery. The BPD-DS changes the hormones in the intestines in a way that makes people feel less hungry, fuller, and better able to control their blood sugar than the gastric bypass and sleeve gastrectomy. Also, the BPD-DS is the most effective metabolic surgery approved by the FDA to treat type 2 diabetes.

Pros

- One of the best ways to cut down on obesity

- Changes the hormones in the gut to make people feel less hungry and fuller after they eat.

- It is one of the best ways to deal with type 2 diabetes.

Cons

- The number of problems is a bit higher than with other surgeries.

- The most malabsorption and the most risk of vitamin and micronutrient deficiencies.

- Heartburn and reflux may get worse or get worse.

- You can have bowel movements that are looser and more regular.

- More difficult surgeries require longer stays in the operating room.

1.2 Health Benefits of Bariatric Surgery

People who get bariatric surgery can lose a lot of weight and keep it off for a long time.

Losing weight and then putting it back on doesn't help much with the health risks that come with being overweight. If you lose weight, you must keep it off for at least five years for it to succeed and make you happier and healthier.

Bariatric surgery is good for more than just losing weight:

Long-Term Remission from Type 2 Diabetes

One study found that type 2 diabetes goes away for a long time after gastric bariatric surgery. The results of this study show that the treatment works very well for obese people with type 2 diabetes. After surgery, almost all of the patients did not need insulin for at least three years.

The State of One's Heart Has Improved

After weight loss surgery, a person is less likely to get heart disease, a stroke, or peripheral heart disease. Also, one study found that weight loss from surgery can lower the risk of dying from a stroke, high blood pressure, or myocardial infarction. Blood pressure and cholesterol levels can go back to normal or almost normal after surgery. This lowers these risks and improves overall health.

Depression Gets Better

Many obese people are sad because they don't like their appearance and because society makes them feel bad about it. Even younger people who are overweight find it hard to do things they might normally enjoy, which can make them feel lonely and depressed. If these people lose weight, it might help their mental health. People who had bariatric surgery had their depression go down by 32.7 percent at the time of surgery and by 16.5 percent six to twelve months later.

Put an End to Obstructive Sleep Apnea

People with sleep apnea can often stop using a CPAP machine at night if they reach and stay at a healthy weight. About 80% to 85% of people who have bariatric surgery no longer have it a year later.

Reduction of Joint Discomfort

Your weight-bearing joints are put under a lot of stress when you are overweight. This can cause long-term pain and joint degeneration. Bariatric surgery causes people to lose a lot of weight and keep it off for a long time. This reduces joint stress and makes it possible for many people to stop taking painkillers and move around a lot better.

Boost Fertility

Women with weight loss surgery could also become more fertile during their childbearing years. One study found that bariatric surgery can lower the risk of miscarriage and help women who don't ovulate get their periods back.

Cuts Down on Other Health Problems

Surgery can help with metabolic syndrome, problems during pregnancy, gallbladder illness, and other health problems.

Since obesity and the health problems that come with it are on the rise, bariatric surgery is a strong way to help overweight people feel better for a long time. When making this choice, it's important to choose a clinic that has a lot of experience with these kinds of operations.

The best facilities have a team of specialists who help patients get ready for surgery and care for them afterward.

"Patients have the best chance of success when a skilled medical team surrounds them made up of surgeons, bariatric medical specialists, nurses, psychiatrists, endocrinologists, and nutritionists."

1.3 Who Should Consider Bariatric Surgery

When you have surgery to lose weight, it changes the way your digestive system looks and works. This surgery might help you shed pounds and deal with health problems caused by being overweight. Conditions like diabetes, obstructive sleep apnea, & high blood pressure and cholesterol levels are examples of these health issues.

Bariatric surgery is another name for weight-loss surgery. There are different kinds of surgeries, but they all help you lose weight by restricting the amount of food you can consume. Few procedures also make it harder for you to take in nutrients.

In the U.S.A, sleeve gastrectomy is the most prevalent surgery for losing weight. During this procedure, a large part of the stomach is removed to make a tube-like sleeve.

Surgery to reduce body fat should be considered as part of a comprehensive strategy to help people slim down. Your procedure will also include advice on how to eat, how to exercise and care for your mental health. To reach your weight-loss goals, you must have the ability and determination to see this plan through to its completion.

If you're thinking about weight-loss surgery, you'll talk to a few experts who can help you in deciding if it's a good idea for you.

You may be a contender for weight loss surgery if you meet the following criteria:

- You're an obese adult, particularly if you have a weight-related situation like type 2 diabetes.

- You are aware of the risks and advantages.

- You're ready to change your eating habits after the surgery.

- You're dedicated to making changes in your lifestyle to maintain your weight loss.

Why is Extra Fat Dangerous?

We may start noticing weight gain in our waist, belly, hips, or neck, but it's what we can't see that puts us at risk for cardiovascular disease. This is because, in addition to accumulating beneath our skin, fat deposits form within our abdomen, between our hearts and the sac that surrounds them, and within our artery walls. Internal fat deposits hasten the formation of atherosclerosis, hypertension, type 2 diabetes and sleep apnea, all of which raise the risk of a heart attack or stroke.

The dangers of being overweight extend further than the cardiovascular and vascular systems. "Obesity is linked to more than half of all cancers in women."

Medical Recommendations

General medical recommendations for bariatric surgery are derived from body mass index (BMI). The body mass index (BMI) is a tool for determining an individual's level of obesity. Surgical weight loss can be helpful for adults with a body mass index (BMI) of 40 or even higher.

Possible candidates for the surgery among adults include those who meet all three of the following conditions:

- Body Mass Index of 35 or even higher

- Obesity-related disease or condition

- Have tried to lose weight under medical supervision for at least 6 months

In few cases, adolescents may benefit from surgical weight loss. Please follow these rules as a guide:

- Medical problems associated with obesity and a body mass index of 40 or even higher

- A serious obesity-related medical issue and/or a (BMI) body mass index of 35 or even higher

Surgeons don't have to use BMI numbers. Instead, they can use growth charts for teens as a guide. These charts show the reasonable levels of (BMI) body mass index for different ages. How much the teen's (BMI) body mass index is higher than the normal will determine whether or not the surgeon recommends the procedure.

Some adults and teens with lower BMIs may be good candidates for weight-loss surgery, depending on the type and severity of an illness caused by obesity.

How to Determine If You're Prepared for Surgery

If you're thinking about having weight-loss surgery, you will encounter with a healthcare team that could contain the following people:

- Primary care physician

- Surgeon

- Anesthesiologist

- Psychiatrist or psychologist

- Dietitian

- Weight management nurse specialist

- Other specialists may be required based on your medical issues.

Members of your group will clarify what to expect during and after the process. They will assess your willingness to undergo surgery and assist you in determining whether it is a viable option for you. They may discover medical, behavioral, or psychological issues that must be addressed before surgery.

Medical Issues

A medical exam will be performed to rule out any undiagnosed obesity-related issues. Your doctor will also look for issues that could complicate surgery. You may be subjected to tests for:

- Obstructive sleep apnea

- Kidney failure

- Cardiovascular illness

- The disease of the liver

If you have any of the following conditions, you will most likely be unable to have surgery:

- Disorders of blood clotting

- Severe disease of heart that makes anesthesia unsafe to use

- Other issues that raise the risk of anesthesia use

Mental Health and Behavior

Weight loss following surgery is dependent on your willingness to alter your habits of eating and exercising. Being in a good mental condition is also crucial for the requirements of adhering to your treatment regimen. The goals of your team are to identify behavioral or psychological risk factors, resolve any issues, and determine whether you are ready for the surgery.

Your medical team will discuss the following topics with you:

- **Motivation:** Do you want to make lifestyle alterations, set your goals, and find out more about nutritious eating? Your team will monitor your capability to implement recommended dietary and exercise changes.

- **Previous attempts at weight loss:** What weight-loss diets and exercise regimens have you tried in the past? Have you lost or gained weight? Weight loss and gain patterns can assist your team comprehend your challenges and recommend post-surgical goals.

- **Eating habits:** Obesity may be exacerbated by irregular eating habits or eating disorders. Nighttime eating, binge eating, and unforeseen grazing between the meals are examples of these. A few eating disorders are linked to other sort of mood disorders and mental health issues.

- **Mood disorders:** Obesity is associated with depression, bipolar disorder, anxiety, and other mood disorders, and these issues can make it hard to handle your weight. Furthermore, individuals with undiagnosed mood disorders frequently struggle to maintain exercise practices and new diet after surgery.

- **The use of alcoholic beverages and drugs:** Poor weight loss and prolonged substance use issues after surgery are linked to troubles with drug or alcohol usage, and smoking. Unmanaged or untreated issues are likely to preclude the choice of weight-loss surgery.

- **Danger of suicide:** Individuals who have had weight-loss surgery are more likely to commit suicide. People suffering from a substance abuse disorder, anxiety, depression, schizophrenia, bipolar disorder, or other disorders are at a higher risk.

Preoperative Expectations

The members of your care team will collaborate with you to devise a treatment plan if they determine that bariatric surgery is necessary. Those things could be:

- **Dietary recommendations:** Vitamin supplements, nutrition guidelines, & menu planning will be provided by the dietitian. Changes during and after the surgery are included in the guidelines.

- **Exercise program:** An occupational therapist, nurse or other specialist will assist you in learning appropriate exercises, making a workout plan, and establishing goals.

- **Weight reduction:** Before having surgery, you may be motivated or need to shed some pounds via exercise and diet.

- **Psychotherapy:** To cure an eating disorder, depression, or other mental health condition, you may be necessitated to start drug treatment, talk therapy, or other sort of mental health therapy.

Constructing new coping mechanisms or addressing concerns about self-esteem or self-image may be part of your therapy.

- **Smoking:** There will be a strong emphasis on getting smokers to either give up the habit entirely or enroll in a smoking-reduction program.

Other therapies: You will be anticipated to adhere to treatment plans for other medical issues.

The goal of these guidelines is to assist you in getting the most out of your weight loss surgery. Finally, demonstrating that you can carry out these action plans will demonstrate to your team that you are committed to doing things properly following surgery. Surgery to reduce body weight may be canceled or delayed if your medical team determines:

- You are not mentally or physically prepared for surgery.

- You haven't altered your diet or exercise routine sufficiently.

- During evaluation, you gained weight.

Surgery Costs

Weight-loss surgery may be covered by your insurance company. Your team must demonstrate that the operation is medically required. You may also be required to give documented proof that you could not lose sufficient weight with a monitored exercise and diet program. The costs may be covered by Medicare as well as some Medicaid plans.

It's vital that you learn as much as possible about your insurance plan and your potential out-of-pocket amounts. A hospital's financial aid office may be able to assist you in exploring different payment plans for your operation.

Can You Benefit from Bariatric Surgery?

Your medical and nursing professionals and other advisors will assist you weigh the pros and cons of this course of action.

You can also access the procedure the clinic uses to decide if you're healthy enough for a weight-loss operation. You'll have to think long and hard about the pros and cons, stick to your pre- and post-op plans, and adopt a new diet and exercise routine.

Chapter 2: Pre and Post-Surgery Food Lifestyle

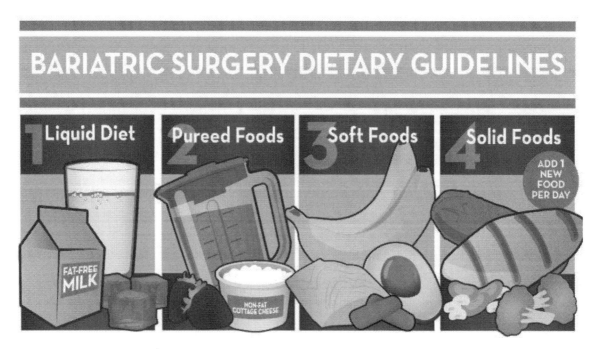

Surgery is only a small part of your weight loss and wellness journey. Your new lifestyle will require practice, time, and dedication, just like learning a new hobby or sport. This chapter will teach you what to eat before and after surgery with tips on eating out to ensure your success.

2.1 The Pre-Surgery Diet

Most patients are required to follow a pre-op diet in order to lose weight and reduce the amount of fat in and around the liver and abdomen prior to surgery. This will reduce the possibility of complications during your procedure and prepare you for a new eating pattern. Your surgical team will determine your exact pre-op guidelines and any required weight-loss goal, but this section provides general pre-operative guidance that will also guide you into post-op living.

2.1.1 Pre-Op Diet Guidelines

Different hospitals and doctors may have different pre-op recommendations. For at least two weeks prior to surgery, you will likely need to adhere to a low-calorie, low-carbohydrate, or liquid diet.

Protein Supplements and Shakes

Protein shakes or powders will be used at some point if you are having bariatric surgery. Protein helps to strengthen and protect muscle tissue while also encouraging your body to burn fat rather than muscle. Protein shakes are an excellent meal replacement option if you are required to follow a liquid diet prior to surgery.

Some commercial protein shakes are high in sugar or have a low protein content per serving. Look for shakes with at least 20 grams of protein per serving that are low in fat and carbohydrates.

To get you started, here are a few protein supplement recommendations:

- **Isolated Whey Protein:** Lactose-free, milk-based protein that is complete (best tolerated and most absorbable for bariatric patients)

- **Soy Protein:** Complete protein derived from plants

- **Egg White Protein:** Non-milk-based, complete protein

- **Whey Protein Concentrate:** Lactose-containing milk-based complete protein (may cause discomfort in gastric bypass patients with lactose intolerance after surgery).

Fat

Prior to surgery, you must be mindful of the amount and type of fat you consume in order to gain control over your caloric intake and lose weight. To find hidden sources of fat, use a food tracking app and read labels.

What to Consume

- Almonds

- Fatty fish (like tuna, salmon, and mackerel)

- Peanuts

- Avocados

- Canola oil

- Olives

- Chia seeds

- Flaxseed

- Walnuts

- Nut butters, all-natural

- Olive oil

- Seafood

What to Avoid

- Baked goods

- Chips

- Animal fats

- Cream sauces

- Foods high in saturated fat

- High-fat condiments (such as mayonnaise)

- Fried foods

- High-fat salad dressings

- Chocolate

- Full-fat dairy products

- Stick margarines containing the hydrogenated oils

- Tropical oils

Sugar

Sugar is a particularly sneaky ingredient that can be found in almost any prepared food you buy. Ketchup, yogurt, dried fruit, barbecue and other sauces, sports drinks, fruit juices, pasta sauce, pre-made soups, frozen dinners, flavored coffees, granola bars, protein bars, and even some protein shakes are high in sugar. Removing sugar from your diet can be difficult, but finding healthier alternatives will aid in weight loss and promote better post-op habits.

High Carbohydrates Foods

Reducing your carbohydrate intake has been shown to help with blood sugar control, craving management, and weight loss. However, giving up carbs is often easier said than done. While going completely carb-free before surgery may not be necessary, it is a good time to make some changes. Try a burger wrapped in lettuce instead of a bun, cauliflower rice in place of white rice, or zucchini noodles in place of pasta noodles.

What to Consume

- Nuts

- Dairy products, low-fat

- Vegetables, non-starchy (like spinach, asparagus, broccoli, onions, cauliflower, kale, and zucchini)

- Seeds

- Whole fruits

What to Avoid

- Chips

- Sweet sauces and dressings

- Corn

- Flour, white (as in breads, pasta, crackers, and tortillas)

- Rice

- Fried foods

- Dried fruit

- Potatoes

Drinks

You may find it difficult to stay hydrated after surgery due to the inability to drink with meals or consume large quantities of fluid quickly. Aim for at least 48 to 64 ounces of hydrating fluids per day prior to surgery. Limit your caffeine intake and avoid beverages high in fat or sugar.

What to Drink

- Water

- Sports drinks, sugar-free

- Water, infused

- Tea, unsweetened

- Broth, low-sodium

- Water, flavored, sugar-free

What to Avoid

- Coffee

- Sodas and other carbonated drinks

- Fruit juices

Habits to Avoid

You will be asked to stop smoking or using tobacco prior to surgery, as both can delay healing and increase your risk of blood clots, pneumonia, and ulcers. You will also be asked to refrain from drinking alcohol for a period of time prior to and following surgery.

2.2 A New Relation with Food

Many patients experience a shift in their relationship with food as a result of surgery. You may have previously reached for food when bored, stressed, or sad, but continuing these habits after surgery may jeopardize your long-term success.

Consider other ways to cope with emotional situations instead of relying on food for comfort. Are you feeling lonely? Make a phone call to a friend. Bored? Take on a project. Stressed? Take a short stroll. Change your focus from what you're eating to what you're doing. Instead of going out to dinner with friends, plan an activity. Food will lose some of its holds on your life over time. Much of your success will be determined by your relationship with food, and you must take the lead in that relationship. Here are some pointers to get you started:

- If you're feeling down, don't turn to food for comfort. Practice emotion-management techniques that do not involve food.

- Instead of trying to grab a midafternoon coffee or pastry "pick-me-up," take a brisk walk during your workday.

- To avoid the lure of less-healthy options, pack meals and snacks to hold with you when running errands.

- Make a shopping list before you go to avoid impulse purchases.

- If you do indulge, don't punish yourself. At your next meal, try to get back on track.

How to Eat

After surgery, how you eat is almost as important as what you eat. Patients tolerate food better when they take small bites, chew their food thoroughly (25 to 30 times), and eat slowly (over the course of 20 to 30 minutes) due to anatomical changes associated with bariatric surgery. You should be finished with your meal in 30 minutes. You should also avoid drinking with meals to avoid filling your pouch with fluid instead of food or having food flush out of your stomach too quickly. Instead, you'll have to drink fluids in between meals.

Patients report a loss of appetite after surgery due to a decrease in ghrelin, the hunger hormone produced primarily by the stomach. It may feel strange to eat when you aren't hungry; consider making a meal plan or setting alarms to remind yourself to eat. Most patients require three to six meals per day to meet their protein and nutrient requirements.

You can prepare for surgery by following these habits. You might even want to start experimenting with some of the recipes in this cookbook. Try meal planning by selecting a few meals and shopping ahead of time.

Here are some ideas to help you reconsider your eating habits:

- Make use of smaller plates and bowls.

- Take tiny bites.

- Chew thoroughly for at least 25 to 30 seconds.

- Consume slowly.

- Keep an eye out for satiety cues, such as a hiccup, sneeze, burp, sigh, or runny nose.

2.3 The Post-Surgery Diet

Your post-op diet will start with liquids, then purées, then soft foods, before returning to normal textures. Protein will be your primary fuel during this healing period. Your doctor will determine the exact length and requirements of each phase of your recovery, but here are some general guidelines to consider:

- **Clear-liquid diet:** This stage typically lasts no more than two days. It enables your care team to assess your liquid tolerance and assists you in practicing frequent hydration.

- **Full-liquid diet:** This stage is designed to maximize your fluid intake and incorporate protein supplements once you have fully tolerated liquids.

- **Purée diet:** Start reintroducing foods to your body. Your body will be able to digest more nutrients and resume proper digestion as you begin to heal. Pay attention to portion sizes and how much food your stomach can safely digest.

- **Soft-foods diet:** You may be able to reduce your reliance on protein shakes and powders as you reintroduce more foods with soft textures into your diet. To meet your dietary goals, eat protein-rich foods as often as possible.

- **General diet:** After you've finished your transitional diet, you can start reintroducing different textures. Continue to pay attention to portion control, eat protein first, and avoid high-fat and high-carb foods.

POST-OP DIET PHASES

	PHASE ONE: FULL LIQUIDS	PHASE TWO: PURÉES	PHASE THREE: SOFT FOODS	PHASE FOUR: GENERAL DIET
ADJUSTABLE GASTRIC BAND	Weeks 1 and 2	Week 3	Week 4	Weeks 5 or 6+
LAPAROSCOPIC SLEEVE GASTRECTOMY	Weeks 1 and 2	Week 3	Weeks 4 to 6	Weeks 7 or 8+
ROUX-EN-Y GASTRIC BYPASS	Weeks 1 and 2	Weeks 3 and 4	Weeks 5 to 8	Week 9+

2.3.1 Phase 1

This phase of your new diet will last approximately one week following your surgery. During this time, people will only drink clear liquids.

The purpose of a clear diet is to prevent postoperative complications such as dehydration, gastric leakage, constipation, diarrhea, and bowel obstruction. Your body needs time to heal, and this phase will help you get there.

Staying hydrated after surgery will help you heal faster and will alleviate symptoms such as vomiting and nausea. While adhering to a clear liquid diet can be difficult, the majority of people will feel very little to no hunger in the days following surgery. You should avoid the following:

- Soda

- Carbonated beverages

- Sugary drinks, such as fruit juice

- Caffeinated beverages such as coffee and black tea.

Sugary drinks can contribute to dumping syndrome, a complication caused by excessive sugar entering the small intestine quickly. This will result in nausea, vomiting, diarrhea, and fatigue. Sugar is nothing more than empty calories. It must be avoided at this time, and in the long run, it should be minimized.

Caffeine can dehydrate you and cause acid reflux. Even non-sugary carbonated beverages can cause bloating and gas. It wouldn't hurt to eliminate carbonated beverages from your diet entirely.

If you're having trouble staying hydrated, consult your doctor and see if they recommend an electrolyte drink, such as low-calorie Gatorade.

Instead, you should drink sugar-free clear liquids. You should also drink at least eight glasses of water per day. This day could include:

- Popsicles with no added sugar

- Decaffeinated coffee or tea

- Broth

- Jello

2.3.2 Phase 2

Most people begin to feel hungry again about a week to ten days after surgery. This is a good sign, but it does not imply that you are ready for solid foods. Your system isn't ready for those yet, which can lead to complications like vomiting. During this time, you will be able to transition to a more complete liquid diet high in protein. During this time, the goal should be to eat a wide variety of healthy nutrients while also avoiding overly sugary foods and foods that have no positive effect on your health.

The following foods should still be avoided:

- Chunky foods, such as vegetable soup

- High-fat foods such as whole-milk yogurt

- Foods high in sugar

During phase two, you should continue to drink plenty of water and incorporate as much protein as possible into your diet. This is typically accomplished by consuming protein powder. Make certain that your protein powder is sugar-free.

Every day, you should aim to consume around 20 grams of protein. At each meal, intake should be limited to about a half-cup of liquid. Sugar-free foods can include the following:

- Water-diluted low-sugar applesauce

- Sugar-free, nonfat yogurt or ice cream

- Very soft soup noodles

- Sugar-free instant breakfasts

- Diluted juice

- Sorbet, pudding, or ice cream without added sugar

- Very thin soups, such as creamed soups

- Nutritional shakes with no added sugar

- Hot cereal that has been thinned, such as oatmeal or cream of wheat

- Unsweetened milk

- No-chunk soups made with thin cream and broth

- Shakes with protein powder

- Instant breakfast beverages

When you reach the end of your second week or the beginning of your third week, it should be safe to begin incorporating pureed and thicker foods. You should still avoid foods that are high in sugar and fat. Processed foods should be avoided at all costs.

In addition to the foods mentioned earlier, you can begin eating the following after the end of your second week:

- Whitefish puree

- Eggs scrambled

- Pureed foods and smoothies, as long as they are sugar-free

- Infant foods

- Pureed tuna or chicken, canned

- Potatoes mashed

- Greek yogurt

- Sweet potatoes mashed

- Thinned oatmeal

During this time, you should aim for 60 to 80 grams of protein per day. Protein is abundant in fish, eggs, and Greek yogurt. It's critical to get enough protein to feel satisfied. Protein can be eaten as the first course of your meal.

Your meals should contain no more than half a cup of liquids. This means that several small meals must be consumed throughout the day.

2.3.3 Phase 3

This is the stage at which you will gradually transition into a soft food phase of your diet. You must continue to consume 60 to 80 grams of protein per day, as well as stay hydrated. On the pureed food diet, you can eat anything, but avoid the following foods:

- White rice and pasta

- Tough, raw vegetables

- Fatty foods such as butter and oil

- Bread

- Seeds and skin from fruits and vegetables

- Foods high in sugar

Consuming a nutrient-dense, high-protein diet of soft foods will help you feel full longer and recover faster. Among the best options are:

- Soups, even if they have small chunks.

- Low-fat deli meat

- Vegetables that have been softened

- Eggs

- Cheese that is low in fat

- Soft fish

- Hummus

- Mashed bananas or extremely ripe mangos

- Fruit canned in natural juices

- Cottage cheese

- Tofu silken

You must continue to drink a daily protein shake and limit the amount of caffeine you consume to one to two cups per day unless your doctor tells you otherwise. It's also a good idea to avoid spicy foods because they can cause heartburn.

2.3.4 Phase 4

This stage occurs about four weeks after surgery. This is the time to start eating solid foods again. Everyone should continue to consume protein shakes and aim for 60 to 80 grams of protein per day. You must stay hydrated, but you must refrain from drinking 30 minutes before you intend to eat. It is a good idea to take a daily bariatric multivitamin if your doctor allows you to. This regimen should revolve around eating three small meals and two small snacks throughout the day. You should avoid snacking on processed or sugary low-fiber foods once again.

Most foods are safe for you to eat at this point. Continue eating the protein-rich foods from earlier phases, and include foods such as:

- A few pieces of fruit

- Fruits and vegetables

- Lean cuts of meat

- Fish

- Cottage cheese (low-fat)

It is best to avoid consuming calories in your beverages. This will leave you feeling less satisfied than eating solid food and may result in nutritional deficiencies. You should avoid the following foods.

- Foods with a lot of calories

- Deep-fried foods

- Desserts

- Sodas

- Desserts

- Cooking fats

- Packed foods such as potato chops

- Snacks high in sugar

- White bread and grains

2.4 Foods to Avoid

Now, from the day of your surgery to a few months later, your doctor will be there to guide you through the various phases and ensure that nothing goes wrong. After that, it is up to you to continue eating wisely, which is where many people fail.

Some bariatric surgery patients will make the mistake of thinking that once they are back on solid foods, they can eat whatever they want. Others believe that certain foods are permanently off the table and that they will have to peruse the baby food aisle indefinitely. Both of these people are incorrect. The majority of patients will be able to tolerate most foods, but they are not always encouraged to do so. The following eight foods should be avoided after surgery, even if you are back on solids.

Foods High in Empty Calories

Because your stomach is the size of an egg after surgery, it requires adequate daily nutrition, which you can achieve by making wise dietary choices. This means you should avoid foods that will hinder your body's recovery after surgery. Popcorn, sweets, rice cakes, chips, pretzels, and pastries fall into this category. If you eat these foods regularly, you may become malnourished or gain weight. Foods high in sugar or that have been fried can result in dumping syndrome. This isn't to say you should avoid them like the plague. You can indulge in a small amount at parties or special occasions as long as you eat healthier foods, and these foods do not constitute the majority of your diet. If you have any, once a month or less is ideal.

Alcohol

Booze is high in calories, and your doctor will advise you to avoid it as part of your post-surgery diet. Alcoholic drinks, like all liquids, will take up important space in your stomach that should be taken up by mineral and vitamin-rich food. Also, alcohol absorption increases dramatically after surgery, which can lead to you becoming intoxicated faster.

Patients are typically advised to drink two liters of water per day or non-caffeinated beverages. It's critical to remember that you shouldn't drink beverages with food for 30 minutes after or before a meal. This is important because it will make you feel fuller and will allow important nutrients to remain in your stomach.

Dry Foods

Because you can't drink liquids while eating, it's probably best to avoid dry foods, at least when you first begin phase four. Granola and nuts, for example, can be difficult to swallow. Regular cereal is fine as long as it is consumed with low-fat milk. When you want to start incorporating some of these foods, start with a very small piece to see if you can tolerate them. Don't be disheartened if you can't. As you continue to heal, you may be able to eat more of these foods.

Bread and Pasta

Because pasta and bread are so starchy, they can form a paste in your throat that is difficult to swallow without some sort of liquid. They can occasionally block the stoma, which is the hold to the pouch that is your stomach. You don't have to completely avoid high-starch foods, but it's a good idea to avoid them at first. When you do consume them, make sure to stick to very small portions and eat in very small bites.

Fibrous Fruits and Vegetables

You should eat plenty of nutritious vegetables and fruits but avoid fibrous vegetables that are difficult to digest. During your first few weeks, you should avoid asparagus, cabbage, broccoli, corn, and celery. You may find that you can tolerate these foods over time, but for now, stick to soft, cooked vegetables with no skin. Peas and beans are excellent choices because they provide your body with the extra protein required to function properly.

Foods High in Fat

Consuming fatty foods immediately after surgery will make you feel nauseous, and they aren't good for long-term weight loss success. Avoid hard cheeses, sausage, whole milk, butter, and bacon in favor of lower-fat alternatives. Low-fat cheese, lean beef, turkey, chicken, and low-fat sandwich meats are all good options. Dumping syndrome can also be caused by eating too much fat.

Caffeinated and Sugary Beverages

Fructose, sugar, and corn syrup should be avoided following surgery. Some fruit juices, as well as all sugary sodas, will result in dumping syndrome. You should instead consume decaffeinated coffee, unsweetened packed drinks, water, and tea. Caffeine causes dehydration, so avoid it while your body adjusts to your new stomach.

Tough Meats

After having surgery, bariatric patients must develop the habit of chewing their food thoroughly. The more you chew, the easier it will be to swallow and digest your food. When eating meat, it is critical to chew thoroughly. Lean meats are important for your diet because they provide a lot of protein. Choose meats with no gristle or fat while you get used to chewing more. Begin with bites about the size of a pencil eraser. Avoid ham, hot dogs, pork chops, and steak. Instead, opt for fish, baked chicken, minced turkey, or chicken.

When it comes to a bariatric diet, there is a steep learning curve. You'll get the hang of it eventually, and there will be no-no foods that you'll later discover you can eat again. Even years after your surgery, listen to your body and follow your doctor's instructions. All of this will help you maintain a healthy relationship with food.

2.5 Choosing the Right Foods

When choosing foods to eat, choose those that are high in protein, low in carbs, and moderate in healthy fats. Foods high in healthy fats include:

- Coconut oil

- Nut butter

- Sardine

- Nuts

- Sailfish

- Avocadoes

A general rule of thumb for selecting foods is:

- Choose very lean meats.

- Canned tuna and salmon.

- Limit your intake of spicy and greasy foods. Spice can be added later on in moderation.

- Avoid using whole milk.

- Eat nutrient-dense foods such as eggs, meats, vegetables, and fruits.

- Make a meal plan.

- Keep your family informed about your healthy eating habits.

- Go grocery shopping for nutritious foods.

- Try to limit or eliminate desserts entirely.

- Avoid temptation by eliminating junk foods.

- Avoid fast food.

- Go out to eat on occasion.

- Take high-quality nutritional vitamins and supplements.

- Separate your food and water by at least 30 minutes.

- Introduce new foods gradually.

- Your meals should be no bigger than the size of your fist.

2.6 Complications

Dumping syndrome is the most prevalent complication that you may experience following surgery, particularly once you begin eating solid foods. Dumping syndrome occurs when sweet or fatty foods are consumed too quickly or in excess.

When this occurs, the stomach dumps the food into the small intestine before it has had time to properly digest it. Dumping syndrome is characterized by nausea, cramps, sweating, diarrhea, vomiting, and increased heart rate. These symptoms usually subside after an hour or two. However, dumping syndrome is extremely unpleasant, so do everything you can to avoid it.

To help reduce your chances of experiencing dumping syndrome, you should:

- Completely chew your food.

- Consume food slowly and steadily.

- Limit your intake of refined carbohydrates and sugary foods.

You will discover that certain foods are more difficult to digest than others, and you should avoid them:

- Beans

- Wine grapes

- Corn

- Nuts

- Shellfish

- Pork

- Whole grains

- Beef

Advice and Directions

Here are some general guidelines and pointers to help you succeed after bariatric surgery.

- Avoid NSAIDs such as naproxen, aspirin, and ibuprofen. These over-the-counter pain relievers may reduce your stomach's natural protective coating.

- Increase the amount of movement in your life. Begin by walking and then progress to other types of exercises you enjoy, such as yoga, dancing, and swimming.

- Discuss supplements and vitamins with your doctor to determine which ones you should take.

- Never drink and eat at the same time.

- To avoid dehydration, drink plenty of water or low-calorie electrolyte drinks.

- Avoid fast food, processed foods, fried foods, and trans fats.

- Avoid high-concentrated sugars.

- Avoid non-nutritional calories.

- Chew and eat slowly.

- Do not overeat because your stomach will stretch and stabilize in size over time.

- Recognize the distinction between physical hunger and emotional or mental appetite.

- When pureeing your foods, use a food processor or blender.

2.7 Restaurant Meals (Tips on What to Eat)

You will not be able to eat at your favorite restaurants again simply because you have had or are having bariatric surgery! We all need a break from the kitchen now and then. All you have to do now is make informed decisions that will provide your body with the nourishment it requires. Continue reading for some helpful hints on how to make outdoor dining less stressful.

The most important thing you can do is conduct extensive research on the restaurant's menu. Find foods that appeal to you while adhering to the healthy and wholesome dietary guidelines required to meet your weight-loss goals. Planning ahead of time will help you resist temptation when you're hungry later. Some restaurants may surprise you with how accommodating they are to your requests!

- Look for grilled, baked, broiled, roasted, steamed, or sautéed items.

- Instead of sausage or beef, substitute lean protein sources such as shrimp, chicken breast, fish, turkey, scallops, mussels, and tofu - and eat your protein first!

- Avoid menu items that are fried, battered, crunchy, tempura, creamy, in a creamy sauce, or alfredo.

- Leave out the bread basket, it will only provide you with empty calories.

- Request roasted vegetables, a side salad, or fruit instead of fries, onion rings, chips, potatoes, or other high-fat/high-carbohydrate sides.

- Request dressings, gravy, sauces, butter, or sour cream on the side, or lime or lemon wedges to add flavor and moisture to your dish to control the addition of calories or sodium.

- Take your time and enjoy each bite while listening to your company's conversation.

- Soups made with broth rather than cream, and vinaigrettes rather than creamy dressings

- Depending on the establishment, appetizers are frequently fried or high-calorie items; however, this is not always the case. Because a healthier appetizer is smaller, it is sometimes preferable to a large entrée.

- Request that your waiter bring you a to-go box with your entrée so you can save half of your food for later or split an entrée with someone else.

Here are a few delicious options from various types of restaurants:

Japanese cuisine: Edamame, sashimi, tuna tartar, seaweed salad, miso soup, ceviche, Naruto sushi roll (no rice, but thin slices of cucumber), and steamed shrimp dumplings

Italian cuisine: Oysters, grilled chicken/salmon/shrimp salad, chef salad, chicken cacciatore, broccoli rabe, grilled veggies, wilted spinach with garlic, grilled calamari, sautéed Swiss chard, broiled/roasted chicken or fish

Chinese cuisine: Hot and sour soup, egg drop soup, egg foo young, mixed vegetables with tofu, shrimp, or chicken, chicken with snow peas, broccoli and chicken, and moo goo gai pan (veggie and chicken stir fry). Sautéed or steamed vegetables and proteins are available in the "healthy" sections of some Chinese restaurants. Sauces are high in sugar and sodium, so request them on the side.

Mexican cuisine: Seafood soup, ceviche, soup, chicken tortilla taco salad (no shell), bowls of burrito without rice, churrasco, siete mares, black beans, salsa, Pescado veracruzano, shrimp or chicken fajitas (no tortilla),

Greek/Mediterranean cuisine: Greek salad, mezze plate, chicken kabobs, red cabbage salad, vegetable hummus, lentil soup, chicken shawarma, tahini salad, Israeli salad, tabbouleh, baba ghanough

Breakfast: Omelets with vegetables, cottage cheese and fresh fruit, and eggs Florentine, Greek yogurt parfaits, fruit-filled oatmeal cups, turkey bacon, poached eggs, fruit cups, turkey sausage, hard-boiled eggs, breakfast low-carb wrap, egg whites

Lastly, pay close attention to how you feel after eating. Do you feel satisfied, confident, and in command? Or are you stuffed, uneasy, and guilty? The more you dine out and have fun, the more certain you are that you are in control and that the food is not controlling you. You don't have to avoid restaurants entirely after surgery, and you can simply enjoy social gatherings without feeling off track.

Chapter 3: Lifestyle Changes

3.1 How to Develop the Proper Mindset to Keep the Weight off

3.1.1 Why Modifying Your Mindset is Essential for Weight Loss?

Making long-term changes requires a shift in mindset. You might be able to convince yourself to work out and enjoy a slightly healthier diet for a few weeks in the short term. However, if you do not have the right mentality for losing weight, you may locate yourself reverting to unhealthy habits. Make a plan to alter your outlook for weight loss if you want to see long-term results. We share eight tips in this part on how to refocus on your weight-loss aims and begin seeing results.

3.1.2 Eight Insider Secrets for Creating a Powerful Mindset for Weight Loss

1. Set Dietary and Fitness Objectives

Having a defined set of attainable goals will assist you in maintaining the proper weight loss mindset. You will be able to set and achieve goals if you have a strong growth mindset and trust that you can achieve what you set your mind to over time. Starting with goals provides you with a strong direction of what you want to accomplish.

Think further than "I want to shed 10 pounds" and aim for a variety of achievable goals, such as:

Being able to bike to work for 25 minutes without stopping

Using tea, coffee, and water instead of soda & sugary drinks

Playing an entire match or round of your favorite games

Understanding how to read food nutrition labels and use them to make healthy decisions

2. Food is Not a Form of Compensation

Food is a sentimental and inspiring reward for many of us. It's all too easy to reach for your preferred comfort food after a long day or to reward yourself for a job well done with a snack. Breaking the link that "food = reward" is critical to changing your weight loss mindset. Once you've trained yourself to feel satisfied by consistently achieving your goals, you'll find it easier to break the habit of comforting or rewarding yourself with food.

3. Don't Classify Foods as "Good" or "Bad"

Similarly, depriving yourself is never a good idea when trying to alter your mindset for the purpose of losing weight. While it's true that some foods are more detrimental to your health than others, it's important to keep your emotions out of the decision-making process when it comes to what you eat. In addition, no matter how "bad" you may think it is, indulging in your favorite foods occasionally is perfectly acceptable. Don't deprive yourself forever of the foods you love, life is about moderation.

4. When You Feel Full, Stop Eating

As a society, we tend to eat our meals far too quickly. If you're trying to get in the mindset to lose weight, eating more slowly and enjoying your food is a great first step. In order to avoid eating too much at meals, it is recommended to take your time. Overeating can be a problem for many people for social or cultural purposes, but it can be avoided if you simply stop eating before you feel full. If you keep eating until you feel full, you will become uncomfortable after you've digested your entire meal.

5. Develop More Self-Control

Discipline oneself to adopt the proper frame of mind to successfully lose weight. Sometimes during this process, you'll have to decline requests from other people. You'll need self-discipline to make the hard decisions, like skipping a family night to go to the gym or passing up doughnuts at work.

Taking away potential sources of temptation is one way to improve one's self-control and make one's journey easier. Instead of driving past your go-to fast food joint on the journey home from work, try taking a different route.

6. To Get Ahead, You Shouldn't Rush

The right frame of mind for weight loss is one marked by patience. It's tempting to check your weight every morning, but if you're easily disheartened by your body's normal ups and downs, you might do better to wait until Friday to do so. Ensure that you allow yourself plenty of time to complete your objectives, regardless of the method you use to monitor your development. Part of having the right attitude to lose weight is embracing that it will take time, as real life, as well as human biology can often stand in the way of weight-loss goals.

7. Keep Moving

To shed pounds, physical activity of any kind is mandatory. While it's true that you can't outrun a bad diet, maintaining an active lifestyle will not only help you get in the right frame of mind to lose weight, but it will also speed up the process. If you want to get in the best shape of your life, it's a good idea to consult with a medical expert about creating a personalized exercise plan that incorporates both cardiovascular (think: running, dancing, and swimming) and strength training activities.

8. If you Want to Lose Weight, Start Keeping a Journal

Keeping a weight-loss journal can assist you to get in the right frame of mind and stay motivated to reach your weight-loss goals. There will be times when you just can't get to the gym or you just can't resist the urge to binge on junk food. Worse yet are the social and family commitments that force you to deviate from your weight loss plan. You can see patterns over time and make necessary adjustments to your weight-loss strategy if you keep a truthful history in your weight-loss journal, which will serve as motivation on the bad days when you feel like giving up.

It's All in Your Head When It Comes to Weight Loss

You need a plan in order to get in the right frame of mind for losing weight. You & your doctor can work out a plan for weight loss if you have realistic goals for your diet and exercise routine. Remember to keep a positive frame of mind. Food is food, and there is no such thing as "bad" or "good" food; it's important to separate your feelings from your eating decisions.

The right frame of mind for weight loss is one in which you take the time to savor your food, discover an activity you can do with enthusiasm, and keep at it with patience and determination. It takes time, but a positive mental attitude and consistent effort can lead to significant weight loss.

3.2 What is Food Addiction and Winning Habits Against Food Addiction

It seems like you're craving everything. There's no reason to feel guilty. Addiction to certain foods has been shown to be a common problem in the real world. Everyone has to deal with it sometimes, so don't feel bad if you're experiencing it too.

An individual's stomach may seem to be the originating point for their food addiction. However, mental factors are the root of any food addiction. That's because it's smart enough to know that certain regions of your brain find high-fat, high-sugar, or high-salt foods to be the most rewarding and pleasurable.

Some foods have been linked to the same brain chemical responses as an addictive drug, according to research. Dopamine is the primary chemical involved here.

Dopamine is one of the most influential and essential chemicals in your body because of this. This substance serves as a communication link between brain cells (also called a neurotransmitter). Further, dopamine is directly involved in locomotion, learning, and digestion. The release of this neurotransmitter is what first gets you out of bed and keeps you focused on finishing the tasks at hand.

However, it also plays a significant role in the development of food addiction as well as cravings. How dopamine contributes to addictive food cravings is as follows: This brain chemical arrives shortly after eating particular foods. Brain dopamine increases activity in reward circuits. Furthermore, your brain craves the opportunity to produce this response once more. That's because your brain is hardwired to seek out and seek satisfaction from experiences like these. And one way your brain can get its fix of reward is through eating certain foods.

People aren't the only sentient beings in the universe. Rats fed a diet of fast food, and other unhealthy snacks developed habits similar to chronic drug users, according to a recent study. When the rats' anxiety was reduced by the dopamine, they craved more junk food. Once the rats developed a tolerance for the high-sugar, high-fat, high-salt, high-carb diet, they refused to eat any other food. According to research conducted in 2009, rats would go so far as to starve themselves while waiting for the junk food that may never arrive.

3.2.1 What to Do to Win...

A quick fix or miracle pill to make you stop craving sugar or other foods is not available. You develop a taste for the things you regularly consume. So… If you want to reduce your cravings, the only thing you can do is take a break. It's only natural to crave dessert after dinner if you have dessert after dinner on a regular basis. It's just a bad habit at this point, though. Like with true drug addiction, fasting certain foods does not increase cravings but rather reduces them, as scientific research has shown.

It takes a lot of effort to alter one's way of life. For this reason, you should make preparations. Here are some ways to curb your food cravings and regain your sense of food security.

Create the Decision to Alter Your Behavior

True transformation necessitates sacrificing some ingrained habits or ways of being in favor of a more desirable alternative. The foods that can wait will have to take a back seat while you focus on your ultimate goal of weight loss or healthier eating habits.

Identify the Precise Factors that Lead to Your Hunger

If you are aware of the circumstances that lead up to your food cravings, you can take preventative measures. If you leave your desk and immediately reach for a chocolate bar whenever you feel stressed, pack your sneakers instead and go for a walk.

Create a Schedule for Your Meals

When trying to alter your diet, it helps to have your meals planned out in advance.

Get Yourself Some Kind of Diversion

This is meant to take the place of your unhealthy eating routine. You see, it's impossible to give up one bad habit without picking up another. Replace dessert or chocolate with flavored herbal tea if you want a sweet treat after dinner. Instead of buying a blueberry muffin or participating in an office bake sale when you're bored, spend that time arranging your meals and workouts for the next week. Get yourself a hobby, maybe.

Put Your Aspirations on Paper and Read Them Frequently

To get what we really want, we sometimes need a gentle nudge in the right direction. If losing weight is your objective, it can be helpful to keep a list of your goals in a conspicuous place, such as the kitchen bulletin board, bathroom mirror, or refrigerator.

Avoid Bringing Tempting Foods into the House

That's an easy one to answer. You can't eat it if it's not on the table.

Encourage Your Loved Ones to Join You

Your close friends and family can be a great resource for keeping you motivated and on track. When attempting major life changes, we need to have someone to hold us accountable. Make sure they are upbeat and motivating and steer clear of those who would encourage you to indulge in junk food.

Food Diaries Can Be Helpful Tools for Weight

We don't consciously control the vast majority of our eating behaviors. Our hectic, multitasking lifestyles have created a major problem: mindless eating. It's easy to overeat or eat when you're not hungry if you eat while doing something else. Keeping a food diary can help you become more conscious of your eating habits by drawing attention to the specifics.

Think Beyond the Food Reward System

Learn to reward yourself in ways other than with food. You can repay yourself with anything from a new outfit to a new book to a relaxing massage without adding any extra pounds, so take the time to relax and plan some nice things you can reward yourself with.

Have a Healthy, Well-Rounded Diet

Dietary fads, severe calorie restriction, and skipping meals all increase the risk of binge eating and weight gain at the next meal. Rather, refrain from doing so. Eat a diet rich in protein, complex carbs, healthy fats, and a wide variety of fruits and vegetables.

Do What You Can to Win the Fight

Food addiction recovery can be arduous and time-consuming. Take it one day at a time and one meal at a time. It's not all bad news, though. You are capable of accomplishing your goals. Moreover, your mindset is an essential weapon in the war on bad attitudes. Expect success and know you deserve it. Afterward, you should initiate baby steps and expand on them.

Once you've pinpointed what sets off your binge-eating episodes, you can replace unhealthy snacks with healthier ones. The ability to resist temptation and urges will soon be yours.

Don't give up hope; that's the most crucial point to keep in mind. You want to make permanent changes to the way you eat and live, so be kind to yourself if you slip back into old ways today and give it another shot tomorrow. The beauty of life is that there is always a second chance.

3.3 Common Mistakes to Avoid People Made After Bariatric Procedures

A permanent solution to obesity, bariatric surgery is an excellent choice. Although it is the most powerful tool for combating obesity, it is not without its challenges. If patients want to see positive outcomes from bariatric surgery, they need to follow instructions and steer clear of the common mistakes.

To be perfect all the time is an impossible standard to meet. Gaining and losing weight after surgery is a process, and there will be challenges. Since we attempt to alter deeply ingrained routines, we need everyone's full attention, cooperation, and cooperation. After having bariatric surgery, many people fall into the following traps:

Assuming You have Recovered

As clichéd as it sounds, surgery is just a means to an end. It will still take effort on your part to keep up with your healthy diet, regular exercise, and vitamin regimen. You must persistently work on overcoming any feelings you have that are connected to food. Weight loss surgery may help, but if you gain the weight back, so will your co-morbid conditions. The decision to have surgery to help you lose weight is the best one you can make, but maintaining your weight loss will take effort.

Having no Nutritional Supplements or Minerals

Vitamins, minerals, and supplements should be taken regularly after bariatric surgery. After surgery, patients must eat a very low-calorie diet and will not be getting all the nutrients they need from food alone; therefore, it is crucial that they take supplements every day to keep adequate levels of minerals and vitamins in the body.

Drinking with the Meals

Overfilling the stomach from drinking fluids with meals can cause discomfort, reflux, or even stretching of your stomach or esophagus, as well as encourage patients to eat more food than necessary and feel hungry sooner.

Not Eating Properly

Maintaining a healthy diet isn't always easy. If we don't use the calories we take in, they get stored as sugar in the body, and if we don't burn that sugar, we get fat. You should focus most of your dietary attention on protein.

Grazing!

Grazing consists of intermittently snacking on small amounts throughout the day. By constantly snacking, your body weight can quickly increase. When you eat small meals and snacks frequently throughout the day, it's easy to lose track of how much you've consumed. In addition to the three square meals daily, sprinkle in some fruit and other healthy snacks as needed.

Lack of Regular Physical Activity!

Exercising on a regular basis is essential if you want to keep off the weight you lose. It is recommended that you work out for 30–40 minutes four times per week. If you find that you can't sustain your exercise for more than 30–40 minutes at a time, don't give up! Can't bear the chill and go for a stroll? You can get in shape by watching an exercise DVD or online videos.

You Aren't Getting Enough Water

It's crucial to drink plenty of water after bariatric surgery. Drinking water can aid in weight loss by facilitating recovery, boosting energy, and enhancing overall performance. Dehydration, which can occur if you forget or ignore to drink water throughout the day, can have negative effects on your health and improvement after weight loss surgery.

Choosing the Wrong Carbs

Processed or repackaged carbohydrates, such as those found in refined or simple carbohydrates, are the worst kind. (For example: cereals, chips, cookies, cakes) Complex carbohydrates, which are typically high in fiber, vitamins, and minerals, are the best option for bariatric patients. (Some examples of such foods include spinach, yams, broccoli, and zucchini.)

Consuming Carbonated Drinks

Soda and seltzer have the ability to increase abdominal distention. If consumed regularly after surgery, the air in carbonated beverages may cause the gastric pouch to expand. In particular, sodas have a lot of sugar that can add up to a lot of calories.

Consumption of Alcohol

Drinking alcohol is a waste of caloric intake. Assuming a gram weighs exactly 7 grams, it would have about 7 calories. Since alcohol is absorbed more quickly in the bloodstream after bariatric surgery, patients should limit alcohol consumption during the weight loss process.

Disregarding the Recommended Serving Sizes When Eating

Follow the instructions for weighing and measuring your food to maximize your chances of long-term success with your weight loss efforts. Roll out the food scale and keep it where you can see it. Keep in mind that a serving size of cooked solid protein (fish, poultry, or meat) that helps you lose weight is 3-4 ounces. Always check the Nutrition Facts labels and have some sort of measuring device on hand.

Major mental and emotional adjustments are necessary before, during, and after surgery. There is no magic bullet for making these modifications, and it takes time to settle into a new routine and diet.

Consequently, blunders are inevitable, but there are usually easy ways to rectify them. Do not forget to consult your dietitian and make use of any and all tools at your disposal. Attend meetings, give speeches, and schedule monthly nutrition appointments!

3.4 How to Deal with Doctors and Nutritionists

Care After Bariatric Surgery

Care following bariatric surgery, or any other procedure to reduce body fat, is crucial.

We share your desire for the best possible results from your bariatric surgery and other weight-reduction efforts. Thus, it is imperative that patients receive follow-up treatment. Patients who consistently show up for their follow-up appointments typically experience greater weight loss than those who don't.

Those who have undergone bariatric surgery often experience varying degrees of success in their recovery. Adjusting to your new weight loss lifestyle is easier if you set reasonable goals for yourself and give yourself time to heal. Successful weight loss requires not only a commitment to a healthy diet and regular exercise but also a supportive social network. Maintaining your weight loss progress can be aided by celebrating your achievements.

Exactly what are the benefits of bariatric follow-up care?

You should keep all of your post-op appointments, as they serve multiple purposes.

- At the time of your release, the likelihood of a successful bariatric procedure is low. Most patients lose weight over the course of 12-18 months following LAP-BAND or sleeve gastrectomy surgery and up to 18-24 months following gastric bypass surgery. You can expect the best possible results from the care and instruction provided afterward.

- Patients who have undergone gastric restrictive surgery can benefit greatly from the guidance of a dietitian who is familiar with managing their recovery. In addition, our dietitian will stress the significance of consuming a healthy, well-balanced diet and staying away from high-calorie liquids & soft foods that can compromise your recovery and surgical success. Just keep in mind that if you continue to eat excessively after your bariatric surgery, the results will be nullified. Specifically, this is true of LAP-BAND surgery. Maintenance of your weight loss progress is facilitated by your follow-up appointments.

- Having you come in for follow-up appointments is also important for spotting vitamin and iron deficiencies early on in your weight loss journey when they are easiest to treat. The risk of developing mineral and vitamin deficiencies increases if post-operative blood tests and follow-up appointments are missed. In cases of severe deficiencies, medical interventions like injections or blood transfusions may be necessary.

Post-operative Appointment Timetable

After surgery, how often do patients need to come in for checkups?

During the first year after surgery, you will likely have four to six follow-up appointments. The frequency of subsequent visits is then set at anywhere from six months to a year.

- **The first visit:** Approximately 2-3 weeks upon bariatric surgery.

- **The second visit:** 4-5 weeks following bariatric surgery. A new solid diet is recommended.

- **Visits every three months:** For the first year following the operation, appointments are scheduled at approximately three-month intervals.

- **Visits on an annual or biannual basis:** After the first year, there will be 6-12 month intervals. The monitoring will continue on an annual basis indefinitely.

Discussing your weight concerns with your doctor at your annual checkup is a great idea. However, there is no harm in setting aside time for a dedicated appointment to address dietary and weight-related concerns.

Tips on How to Talk to Your Doctor

It's always best to take charge of your health and wellness, and medical professionals value patients who do so.

Discussing your weight concerns with your doctor at your annual checkup is a great idea. However, there is no harm in setting aside time for a dedicated appointment to address dietary and weight-related concerns.

You might want to do some reading or research before your meeting so that you can be more productive. Things to consider include the following:

- **Plan ahead:** How much weight do you hope to shed, and for how long?

- **Know your own capabilities and limitations:** Weight loss of 5–10% of your current weight is a reasonable objective. More than that could be counterproductive. Your doctor can help you arrive at a practical plan that can give better long-term results.

- **Don't be shy — initiate the discussion:** There are doctors who might be afraid to bring up their patients' weight for fear of upsetting them. Maybe it was a touchy subject during an earlier appointment with you or another patient. Medical professionals may also avoid discussing weight management because they lack confidence in their ability to counsel patients.

- **Never let yourself be put off by statistics or caught up in classifications:** Any conversation about weight will inevitably involve pounds, body mass index, waist circumference, and terms like "overweight" and "obesity."

- **Discuss the importance of a healthy diet and regular exercise:** In most cases, altering multiple aspects of one's routine is necessary for sustained achievement. Try to come up with some ideas for how you can ramp up your physical activity before your scheduled appointment. If you have a pedometer, track your average daily step count so that you have something to strive toward. Get a "prescription" for workout from your doctor. This strategy will be recorded in your medical record and reviewed at subsequent appointments.

- **Please bring in your food log:** A good estimate would be two or three days' worth of food and drink consumption, broken down by type and quantity. Keeping a diary can help you and your doctor stays on the same page regarding your health and weight loss goals. A written diary will provide more detail and accuracy than a verbal account of one's eating habits. Get a list of recommended foods or a handout from your doctor outlining what you must be eating. A referral to a dietitian or nutritionist may also be made.

Short on time before your doctor's appointment? Then, at the very least, prepare yourself to have an open conversation.

Keep in mind that maintaining a healthy weight is important for your overall health. Give yourself plenty of time to reach your objectives, and enlist the help of those around you, whether that's your family or friends.

3.5 Basic Physical Exercises After Bariatric Surgery

Numerous bariatric surgeries and procedures can be effective in helping people lose weight, but they cannot work miracles. After bariatric surgery, patients need to commit to major lifestyle changes like eating better and exercising regularly if they want to see positive results and move forward with their lives. Those who are willing to stick to a routine and exercise after bariatric surgery will reap many benefits.

A minimum of 2.5 hours of exercise per week is recommended. Distribute this over the course of two to four days. If you want to succeed in the long run, physical activity is a must. Regular exercisers are more likely to maintain their weight loss over time. They'll gain a ton of advantages, both psychologically and physically.

When do I start seeing results from my workouts, and how often should I go? One study found that people who exercised for two and a half hours per week lost 5.7% more weight than those who did not.

If you exercise regularly after surgery, you will recover more quickly and be in better shape. Set aside time to exercise at regular intervals on a regular schedule to keep yourself on track.

Make an effort to disperse your weekly two-and-a-half-hour commitment across three or four days. Exercise for at least half an hour every day, preferably more. This makes it easier to get started each day and allows you to increase your stamina.

Your daily routine ought to be geared toward three objectives:

- During a strength training session, you may use exercise balls, weights, and yoga poses.

- An effective stretching routine is essential for maintaining flexibility. Because of its emphasis on using one's own body weight for resistance exercises and breathing techniques, yoga is also applicable here.

- Long-distance activities like swimming, cycling, and walking.

It's important to exercise carefully after surgery, focusing on three specific areas.

- Cardio

- Flexibility

- Strength training

Let's check off each one of these together.

Flexibility and Stretching

Exercises that increase flexibility, such as stretching, can reduce the risk of injury during other types of physical activity, such as running or weightlifting. After bariatric surgery, your muscles will benefit from increased flexibility exercise because more blood will be flowing to them. More range of motion and less tightness in the tendons are two additional benefits. Just like you see professional athletes do before a big game or competition, you can boost your performance by stretching. It's crucial that you're following a routine that's appropriate for your needs and that you're doing it properly.

If you work with a physical therapist, you can develop a program that will increase in difficulty as your strength increases.

Cardio

Doing cardio regularly increases your metabolism and helps you burn more fat. It can also make you feel more confident and happy, help you sleep better, and reduce your anxiety. The earlier discussed endorphins are responsible for this effect. Cardio improves our mental clarity and physical endurance.

Aerobic exercise can take the form of anything from strolling to swimming to jogging to mountain climbing. Calories are burned when doing cardio, which leads to weight loss. While the precise number will vary from person to person, it generally takes burning 3,500 more calories than you take in per day to drop 1 pound. Therefore, in order to lose a pound in a week, many people may need to reduce their caloric intake by 500 per day. Either reducing caloric intake (by eating less) or increasing caloric expenditure will help you lose fat, but the combination of the two is optimal. Here are a few illustrations to help you visualize it:

- Burning 83 calories in 20 minutes at a pace of 2 miles per hour,

- Twenty minutes of cleaning up the house use up 63 calories,

- The average person can burn 124 calories in 20 minutes of moderate basketball play,

- In order to lose 245 calories in 20 minutes, try jumping rope.

Here are some recommendations to help you get around mobility issues and increase your level of physical activity:

- **Get up and go:** Cleaning your house, parking further away from the grocery store, and taking the stairs instead of the elevator are all easy ways to gradually increase your activity level.

- **Put on your shoes and take a walk:** To ease into a long distance, try starting out with a shorter one.

- **Perform some light aerobic exercises:** There is no requirement for intensity in these routines; rather, duration of motion and frequency of repetitions should be prioritized.

- **You could try something like yoga or Pilates:** It's recommended to begin with chair yoga. If you have trouble moving around or have joint pain, doing these actions while seated may be more manageable.

Strength/Weight Training

In addition to fat, muscle is lost during rapid weight loss. Muscle loss can be mitigated, and new muscle can be built with regular strength training. Having more muscle mass increases your metabolism and helps you burn calories more quickly. Toning muscles through strength training is another way in which core strength can be improved. Some examples of strength-building activities are:

- Lifting weights,

- Sit-ups,

- Lunges,

- Crunches.

- Squats,

After incorporating strength training into your routine, you can gradually increase the intensity of your workouts.

To get you started, We've included a few exercises for each muscle group.

Workouts that focus on the upper body include:

- Modified pushups

- Chest presses

- Overhead triceps extensions

- Chest flies

- Light curls

- Lateral and frontal raises

Consider the following for your lower body:

- Squats

- Glute bridges

- Forward, lateral & reverse lunges

- Wall-sits

- Calf raises

- Jumping jacks

You'll learn over time that certain moves are more beneficial to your health than others. Heavy deadlifts and other weighted exercises can be added to your routine, but you should perfect your form before increasing the weight on your barbell.

How Soon After Bariatric Surgery Can You Work Out?

After having bariatric surgery, many people wonder when they can begin exercising again. What follows is a general description of what you can count on:

- **The immediate period following surgical procedure:** In a nutshell, your exercise routine will begin as soon as possible, and you'll be up and moving around the recovery room. To keep the blood moving and avoid clotting, you'll be doing this, which will also make up the bulk of your exercise routine for the next few weeks. A personalized program outlining a safe post-operative activity and exercise plan will be developed for you and provided to you by your medical team. You'll need to take it easy at first while your body heals, but walking is the first exercise you'll be given to do.

- **In two to four weeks:** Some gentle stretches and flexibility exercises, like shoulder rolls, hamstring stretches, arm rotations, etc., will be incorporated into your regular workout routine. You'll gradually extend the duration of your strolls and may even speed up a bit.

- **By the time you reach 5-6 weeks:** Your body is getting stronger and healthier, so start doing cardio! You should start exercising at least five days a week for thirty min a day under your doctor's supervision. Exercises that are easier on the joints, such as those performed in water or on a bicycle, are good options, but your surgical staff can make specific recommendations for you.

- **When you reach the 7-8-week point:** Two days a week of strength training is where it's at. After having bariatric surgery, some of the best exercises are squats, lunges, and weightlifting. If your doctor has told you to stop doing something and it's causing you pain, you should listen to that advice. You want to "feel a burn," but you should be mindful of your limits. Stop immediately and consult your doctor if you experience any symptoms of nausea, chest pain, or unusual shortness of breath.

You'll keep doing these foundational types of exercise but eventually ramp up the duration and difficulty of your routines. Remember that your body will automatically adapt to your level of activity and that you will burn fewer calories even if you maintain the same exercise routine. As you progress, you'll need to keep nudging yourself to do just a little bit more.

3.6 How to Make 365 Days (Yearly) Meal Plan

When you're already trying to juggle work, family, & social obligations, coming up with what to eat each day can be a source of added stress. It's not uncommon for people to scrounge together an unhealthy meal at the last minute or give up and order takeout.

Planned meals are a better option for feeding yourself and your loved ones. This method guarantees that you will never go hungry again.

What Is the Meal Planning?

Creating a weekly, monthly or yearly menu that is tailored to your dietary preferences is known as meal planning.

When it comes to goals like weight loss or better cholesterol levels, some people choose to follow a predetermined meal plan. Another strategy is meal planning, which can give an athlete the energy and nutrients they need to give their best performance.

Meal packages come in a variety of shapes and sizes. Some may be designed to help with the symptoms of a certain illness, like type 2 diabetes or high blood pressure. When developing one of these plans, it's common practice to consult with a dietitian or medical professional. To keep their blood sugar levels under control, people with type 2 diabetes often adhere to a diabetes-friendly meal plan, while those worried about their heart health due to a family history of the disease might follow a meal plan geared toward heart health.

When not attempting to control a medical condition, most people create their own meal plans by choosing healthy recipes that everyone in the family enjoys.

The Benefits of Meal Preparation Plans

There are several benefits to preparing meals in advance. Meal planning is helpful for everyone because "it's a really nice method to get planned and have some kind of road map for the year."

Planning out your meals for the week ahead requires some time and effort upfront, but once you have everything set, you won't have to worry about what to make for dinner each night. People with demanding schedules, chronic conditions like diabetes, or families to provide for may benefit most from this. A meal plan can alleviate some of the burdens of grocery shopping and cooking by providing a general framework within which to work.

In addition to assisting you in maintaining a healthy weight, meal planning can also assist you in eating more healthfully. Without a plan, "you may be more willing to order a pizza on a hectic evening, even if it's not something you're going to truly enjoy." In contrast, if you have a well-balanced meal waiting for you at home, the thought of ordering pizza or hitting the drive-thru might not sound quite as appealing.

People with health conditions that necessitate careful attention to what they eat, such as those with type 2 diabetes or heart disease, can benefit greatly from adopting a healthier diet. They may find it easier to eat healthily if they have a plan laid out for them. You don't have to worry about whether or not something goes with something else, and you can rest assured that your doctor or dietitian has given the green light for these foods to help you manage your condition.

The problem is that shoppers who don't come up with a game plan end up with a random assortment of ingredients and no clear idea of how to use them. That food will just go bad in your fridge or pantry until you finally get around to throwing it away. But if you make a meal plan, you'll know exactly what and how much to buy, resulting in less wasted food (and cash).

3.6.1 Steps to Make 365 Days Meal Plan

Make Categories

Start up your preferred spreadsheet application. The goal of the first sheet is to generate as many ideas as possible for dinner. Let's simplify the situation a little bit.

Create a menu with seven distinct food types. The seven groups can be about anything; for instance, you could group dishes by their preparation style:

- Sunday: simmer (think of soups and stews)

- Monday: bake (can be roasted?)

- Tuesday: tacos (it is Tuesday, after all)

- Wednesday: bbq (you can go through the bbq recipes and find those you like)

- Thursday: stir-fry

- Friday: slow cooker (pulled pork or other meals)

- Saturday: microwave

A different approach? One option is to embrace stereotypes and try international cuisines:

- Sunday: Italian

- Monday: Chinese

- Tuesday: still Tacos

- Wednesday: American

- Thursday: Polish

- Friday: Thai

- Saturday: … Your Favorite Cuisines out of this book

The combination of meats and meal types is the easiest to categorize and plan for.

- On the weekend, we eat soup.

- On Mondays, we eat our leftovers.

- Meat on a Tuesday, please!

- Served on Wednesdays, chicken

- Thursday: Pork

- Slow Cooker Day Is On Friday

- Saturday: Various.

- And yes, Miscellaneous.

Fish originally occupied the slot of Saturday night dinner. First, we put Vegetarian, then Miscellaneous, and now we are happy with it.

Rotation Between Breakfast, Lunch and Snack

Our Monday routine includes the same morning meal, midday meal, and afternoon snack. On Tuesdays, we do the same thing, and so on.

These meals are on a Seven-day rotation.

This is easy to understand. There's no need for deliberation; everybody is already aware of the meal plan.

Think of Some Dinner Ideas

Once you've decided on your seven groups, use those names as the column headers for your spreadsheet, and get ready for some more entertaining brainstorming (probably inspired by the hilarious Netflix show you've selected).

Make a list with as many dinner options as you can think of under each heading. To avoid eating the same thing more than four or five times a year, limit yourself to a total of 12 meals in each category.

For Instance, on Sundays, it's Soup or Salad Day!

Choose the soup or salad recipes from the recipe sections!

There are distinct salads and soups here in the book. Each of the four or five salads you can plan to make this year will be made on the weekly schedule. However, please note that these are merely suggestions in case you find yourself at a loss. Most likely, the soup or salad you make each week will be "this is what you found inside the vegetable crisper," consisting of whatever vegetables and herbs you happen to have on hand. That's always a plus.

Depending on your perspective, some of the subcategories may be simpler than others. Here are just a few examples:

- spare ribs

- pork fajitas

- pulled pork (which you can actually bump into the slow cooker Fridays)

- pork chops

- ham

That's fine, by the way. Since you'll be looping through each subcategory separately, the length of the lists there is irrelevant.

As a piece of advice, it's preferable to have a short list of meals that you can confidently make than a long list filled with just random recipes.

That doesn't mean you can't try new things when cooking, if you're in the mood for something different, by all means, cancel your planned meal. However, the point of this diet is to help you relax and unwind.

Incorporating complicated recipes into your weekly menu can be counterproductive.

Dinners that are simple or at least routine will be easier to prepare on days when you have less energy.

Start with dinner and then move on to lunch and breakfast. We recommend coming up with one breakfast and one lunch idea for each day of the week, and that's it for these lists.

Produce the Master Checklist

Once you're content with how your week is shaping up, you can start working on your master list. Enter "Date," "Breakfast," "Lunch," and "Supper" at the top of a new sheet of paper. In the fifth column, labeled "Notes," keep track of any online resources you want to include in your research. To put it another way, this is extremely rare.

Dates from now through the end of the year should be entered in the first column. Don't fret; it won't take more than a second. First, enter January 1, 2024 (or the date you'd like to use) into the spreadsheet cell in question, and then use the fill handle to move the date down, down, down to December 31.

The next step is to paste in all of your fantastic menu suggestions.

First, paste your breakfast ideas for the first week into your master list. Repeat this process for the following week and the week after that. Use this method until the end of the year. Take the same approach with your midday meal.

Now for the supper. To fill in the first Sunday cell on the master list, copy the first item in your Sunday category (in our case, soup) and paste it there. The next time you need to add something to your master list on Sunday, just copy the second item in that section and paste it into the empty cell after it. Are you following what we are trying to say here? On Sundays, you will paste the meals from the first category. There will be a lot of back and forth, but eventually you will find a groove.

If you want to keep copying and pasting till you reach by the end of the year, just start at the beginning of your category's list and work your way down. Proceed to the following group. Make a list of the meals you've come up with, and add them one by one.

Some Advice:

- You are free to switch up the meal schedule a little while away. For Instance, during the colder months making it a point to paste out the chilies & stews more frequently, while avoiding them altogether during the warmer months.

- You may also find that sticking to a particular meal (protein sources, duh) on a regular basis is beneficial. When making an annual menu plan, paste salads, for example, every other Tuesday and then fill in the rest of the blanks with other meals from the category.

- The converse is also true; you may wish to reduce the frequency with which you consume a particular meal. That's Rack of Spare Ribs for us! Not only do we not have a lot of money in the Pork category, but we also cannot afford to consume spare ribs each single month.

If you eat the same things every day of the year, you might be wondering how you can start eating seasonally. That's never been an issue because you can always make sure to use whatever seasonal fruits and vegetables are on sale. For Instance, in the winter, you might add mashed sweet potato with cinnamon to chicken wraps, but in the summer, switch to mango as a garnish. That's the best you will ever have! With Chipotle Aioli from Epicure.

Get a Copy of Your Superb Menu Plan

We guess you could print out the entire list and post it to your fridge, but that seems excessive. Instead, you can use a pretty page's template to copy and paste seven days' worth of meals and print that out.

You can either go paperless & read your meal plan on a screen, or you can write it out on a laminated sheet and use it week after week. Use your best judgment.

Also, you shouldn't feel tied down to the timetable. It's just a tool to make things easier; if you don't feel like eating what's on the list one day, don't.

Tips for Establishing a Diet Plan that Spans an Entire Year

- Acquire a binder, some plastic sheet protectors, some dividers, and some tabs.

- Estimate the number of meals you will need each month.

- You should try to find that many recipes that everyone in your family enjoys.

- Place the recipes in the binder, labeling each week.

- Just think how easy it is! Only 28 dishes/recipes (or enough food for four weeks) are needed.

- Plan on having leftovers once a week to begin with. You're down to your last 24 meals now.

- Start by compiling a list of everyone's preferred dishes. Record twenty-four of their most beloved dishes.

- You can cut costs even more by eating the same things week after week.

- You only need 16 more meal ideas if you regularly eat Mexican food on Tuesdays; doing so adds four more meals to your monthly total.

- The best time to make a grocery list is at the start of each week after you've gone through your recipes and determined what you'll need.

Some Suggestions on Balanced Meal Planning for the Whole Year

- Be sure to rotate your protein sources weekly.

- Seasonal vegetables should be rotated weekly.

- Make sure to alternate between simple and complex meals throughout the week.

- Maintain consistency by using the same ingredients every week. Foods that feature cilantro or any other ingredient that isn't typically used in its entirety in a single meal.

- Find out how many lunches you'll need, and cook enough dinners for that many days' worth of lunches.

- Ideally, each meal would consist of a protein, a vegetable, and a grain.

- Fresh, seasonal produce should be the focus of your meal planning this spring and summer. Fresh herbs and produce from your own garden can now be used.

- Plan on using seasonal vegetables and hearty dishes for the upcoming fall and winter months.

Now is the time to make soup in the crockpot or Dutch oven, season it with fragrant herbs and spices, and serve yourself and your loved ones some healthy, hearty comfort food.

Chapter 4: Early Post-Operation Recipes

1. Almond Caramel Protein Shake

Preparation time: 1 minute | **Cooking time:** 0 minutes | **Servings:** 1

Ingredients:

- 1/2 teaspoon of caramel extract

- 1 cup of water

- 1/4 cup of cottage cheese low-fat

- 1 scoop of whey vanilla protein powder

- 1/2 teaspoon of almond extract

Instructions:

- All of the ingredients should be combined inside a blender and blended on high till smooth.

Nutrition Per Serving: Calories 145, Total Fat 1g, Protein 29g, Carbs 6g, Fiber 0.6g Cholesterol 23mg, Sodium 171mg, Potassium 163mg, Phosphorus 71mg

2. Aromatic Infused Chicken Broth

Preparation time: 5 minutes | **Cooking time:** 20 minutes | **Servings:** 2

Ingredients:

- 1/2 cup of onion chopped

- 2 cups of chicken broth store-bought

- 1/2 cup of celery chopped

- 1/2 cup of carrots chopped

Instructions:

- Place all of the ingredients inside a pot and heat over high flame.

- When it begins to boil, reduce the flame to low and leave it to simmer for about 20 minutes.

- Remove the pot from the flame. Set a colander over a dish to drain the broth.

Nutrition Per Serving: Calories 10, Total Fat 1g, Protein 1g, Carbs 1g, Fiber 2g Cholesterol 8mg, Sodium 807mg, Potassium 388mg, Phosphorus 123mg

3. Berry Cheesecake Smoothie

Preparation time: 10 minutes | **Cooking time:** 0 minutes | **Servings:** 2

Ingredients:

- 1 cup of mixed berries

- 2 cups of skim milk

- 4 tablespoons of cream cheese

- 8 to 10 ice cubes

- 1/4 teaspoon of vanilla extract

Instructions:

- All of the ingredients should be combined inside a blender container before being pulsed till creamy.

- Pour into two large glasses to serve. Enjoy!

Nutrition Per Serving: Calories 182, Total Fat 5g, Protein 10g, Carbs 21g, Fiber 3g Cholesterol 6mg, Sodium 214mg, Potassium 433mg, Phosphorus 100mg

4. Blueberry and Spinach Smoothie

Preparation time: 10 minutes | **Cooking time**: 0 minutes | **Servings:** 2

Ingredients:

- 2 cups of blueberries

- Juice of 1 lemon

- 1-inch of fresh ginger, grated

- 3 cups of chopped fresh spinach

- ½ cup of chopped fresh coriander

Instructions:

- Blend all of the ingredients for two minutes with 2 cups of water, or till completely smooth.

- Serve immediately.

Nutrition Per Serving: Calories 121, Total Fat 1g, Protein 2g, Carbs 21g, Fiber 2.6g Cholesterol 6mg, Sodium 214mg, Potassium 147mg, Phosphorus 72mg

5. Chicken Buffalo Salad

Preparation time: 10 minutes | **Cooking time**: 0 minute | **Servings:** 4

Ingredients:

- 1/2 teaspoon of onion powder

- 2 cups of cooked and shredded chicken breast, season with salt & pepper

- 3 tablespoons of buffalo sauce

- 1/4 cup of light mayo

Instructions:

- Combine all of the ingredients, except the celery stems, inside a mixing bowl. Season using salt and pepper to taste.

Nutrition Per Serving: Calories 104, Total Fat 3g, Protein 17g, Carbs 1g, Fiber 0.6mg, Cholesterol 11mg, Sodium 268mg, Potassium 404mg, Phosphorus 244mg

6. Celery Soup

Preparation time: 10 minutes | **Cooking time:** 15 minutes | **Servings:** 2

Ingredients:

- 3 tablespoons of almonds, chopped
- 5 celery stalks, chopped
- 3 cups of vegetable stock
- Black pepper as required
- Salt as required

Instructions:

- Add stock to a pot and bring to boil over high flame for two minutes.
- After adding the celery, cook for about 8 minutes.
- Remove from the flame and purée with an immersion blender till smooth.
- After adding the almonds, thoroughly mix them in.
- Season using salt and pepper to taste.
- After serving, relax and enjoy.

Nutrition Per Serving: Calories 80, Total Fat 6g, Protein 3g, Carbs 5g, Fiber 1g Cholesterol 10mg, Sodium 542mg, Potassium 272mg, Phosphorus 112mg

7. Clear Miso Soup

Preparation time: 5 minutes | **Cooking time:** 20 minutes | **Servings:** 2

Ingredients:

- 1 teaspoon of dashi granules
- 2 cups of water
- 1/2 package of silken tofu diced (8 ounces)
- 1 sliced green onion
- 1 1/2 tablespoons of miso paste

Instructions:

1. Bring dashi granules and water to boil inside a pot over a medium-high flame. Reduce the temperature to medium while whisking continuously and add the miso paste. Tofu should be included. After removing the layers from the green onions, add them to the soup. Separate the liquid from the solids using a filter. Before serving, simmer for two to three minutes over a low flame.

Nutrition Per Serving: Calories 63, Total Fat 2g, Protein 5g, Carbs 5g, Fiber 1g Cholesterol 0.1mg, Sodium 721mg, Potassium 95mg, Phosphorus 41mg

8. Classic Pureed Egg Salad

Preparation time: 10 minutes | **Cooking time:** 0 minute | **Servings:** 2 (1/4 cup)

Ingredients:

*   1 tablespoon of plain Greek yogurt

*   2 hard-boiled eggs

*   1 tablespoon of low-fat mayonnaise

*   Salt and black pepper to taste

Instructions:

*   Halve two hard-boiled eggs.

*   In a food processor, pulse the egg slices till smooth.

*   Process the eggs till there are no large chunks left.

*   Combine chopped eggs, mayonnaise, Greek yogurt, and seasonings.

*   Blend the egg salad till it is completely smooth.

Nutrition Per Serving: Calories 176, Total Fat 13.2g, Protein 9.3g, Carbs 4.6g, Fiber 1g, Cholesterol 43mg, Sodium 267mg, Potassium 550mg, Phosphorus 386mg

9. Chocolate Avocado Mousse

Preparation time: 10 minutes | **Cooking time:** 0 minutes | **Servings:** 2

Ingredients:

- 1/2 tablespoon of cocoa powder

- 1/2 avocado medium

- 20g of whey protein concentrate

- 1/2 tablespoon of maple syrup

Instructions:

- Blend all of the ingredients inside a blender or with a stick blender till smooth.

- Before serving, divide the contents among shot glasses.

Nutrition Per Serving: Calories 87, Total Fat 8g, Protein 1g, Carbs 8g, Fiber 1.2g Cholesterol 83mg, Sodium 77mg, Potassium 289mg, Phosphorus 172mg

10. Cheesy Herb Omelet

Preparation time: 5 minutes | **Cooking time:** 10 minutes | **Servings:** 1

Ingredients:

- 1 teaspoon of oil

- 1 pinch of onion powder

- 1 large egg

- 20g of a grated cheese- 1 slice

- 1 pinch of dried thyme

Instructions:

- With a fork, combine the onion powder, egg, and dried thyme inside a small-sized mixing bowl.

- Inside a small-sized saucepan, heat the oil and add the whisked egg, making sure it reaches all corners. Cook for a few minutes or till the egg is nearly cooked. Serve with a slice of cheese on top. Allow it to simmer briefly to warm the cheese before folding it in half and serving.

Nutrition Per Serving: Calories 201, Total Fat 16g, Protein 12g, Carbs 2g, Fiber 3g, Cholesterol 15mg, Sodium 470mg, Potassium 100mg, Phosphorus 64mg

11. Chocolate Peanut Butter Protein Shake

Preparation time: 10 minutes | **Cooking time:** 0 minutes | **Servings:** 2

Ingredients:

- 2 tablespoons of peanut butter
- 1 tablespoon of cocoa powder unsweetened
- 2/3 cup of water
- 1/2 cup of plain Greek yogurt fat-free
- 1 scoop of chocolate whey protein powder

Instructions:

- Blend all of the ingredients in a powerful blender till completely smooth.

Nutrition Per Serving: Calories 95, Total Fat 1g, Protein 19g, Carbs 5g, Fiber 3g Cholesterol 12mg, Sodium 212mg, Potassium 528mg, Phosphorus 233mg

12. Egg White Scramble

Preparation time: 5 minutes | **Cooking time:** 10 minutes | **Servings:** 2

Ingredients:

- 1/4 cup of non-fat cottage cheese
- Salt & freshly ground black pepper to taste
- 2 egg whites (lightly beaten)
- Pinch of dried herbs (such as oregano or basil)
- Nonstick cooking spray

Instructions:

- Using a fork, break up the cottage cheese into curds inside a medium-sized dish. After adding the egg whites, blend them in.
- Cooking Spray a small nonstick skillet using cooking spray and heat it over medium flame. Add the egg mixture, sprinkle with herbs, and gently stir for 4 to 5 minutes or till thoroughly cooked.
- Mash the cooked egg mixture with a fork to the desired consistency. Season with salt and pepper to taste, and serve immediately. Enjoy!

Nutrition Per Serving: Calories 85, Total Fat 1g, Protein 15g, Carbs 2g, Fiber 0g Cholesterol 5mg, Sodium 55mg, Potassium 54mg, Phosphorus 21mg

13. Easy Chocolate and Orange Pudding

Preparation time: 10 minutes | **Cooking time:** 0 minutes | **Servings:** 2

Ingredients:

- 1 package of sugar-free instant chocolate pudding mix

- ¼ cup of chocolate protein powder

- 1 tablespoon of cocoa powder

- 2 cups of low-fat milk

- 1 teaspoon of orange extract

Instructions:

- Inside a small-sized mixing bowl, whisk together the pudding, protein powders, and milk for 2 minutes.

- Mix for three minutes more before adding the cocoa powder and orange extract.

Nutrition Per Serving: Calories 111, Total Fat 2g, Protein 10g, Carbs 15g, Fiber 1g Cholesterol 0mg, Sodium 17mg, Potassium 30mg, Phosphorus 14mg

14. Grape Juice

Preparation time: 10 minutes | **Cooking time:** 0 minutes | **Servings:** 2

Ingredients:

- ½ lime

- 2 cups of seedless red grapes

- 2 cups of spring water

Instructions:

- Blend all of the ingredients inside a blender till smooth.

- The juice should be strained and divided between two glasses using a strainer.

- Serve immediately.

Nutrition Per Serving: Calories 63, Total Fat 0.1g, Protein 0.6g, Carbs 16g, Fiber 0.5g Cholesterol 0mg, Sodium 13mg, Potassium 263mg, Phosphorus 0mg

15. Guava Smoothie

Preparation time: 10 minutes | **Cooking time:** 0 minutes | **Servings:** 2

Ingredients:

- 1 cup of baby spinach, finely chopped

- 1 banana, peeled and sliced

- 1 cup of guava, seeds removed, chopped

- ½ medium-sized mango, peeled and chopped

- 1 teaspoon of fresh ginger, grated

Instructions:

- After peeling, cut the guava in half. After scooping out the seeds, wash them. Set aside after slicing into small pieces.

- Rinse the baby spinach thoroughly under cold running water. Drain thoroughly before tearing it into small pieces. Set aside.

- Bananas should be peeled and cut into small pieces before cooking. Set aside.

- Mangoes should be peeled and cut into small pieces before cooking. Set aside.

- Inside a juicer, juice the following ingredients: guava, baby spinach, banana, ginger, and mango. While blending, gradually add water till fully combined and creamy.

- Transfer to a serving glass and chill for 20 minutes before serving.

- Enjoy!

Nutrition Per Serving: Calories 166, Total Fat 2g, Protein 5g, Carbs 39g, Fiber 3g Cholesterol mg, Sodium 1.2 mg, Potassium 230mg, Phosphorus 78mg

16. Hot Cream Cocoa

Preparation time: 5 minutes | **Cooking time:** 2 minutes | **Servings:** 1

Ingredients:

- 2/3 cup of vanilla almond milk unsweetened
- 1 tablespoon of no sugar added Dutch-processed cocoa
- 2 tablespoons of no-calorie natural sweetener

Instructions:

- Inside a cup, combine cocoa and sweetener. Almond milk is added and whisked in.
- Microwave on high for 60 seconds. Recombine the ingredients. Microwave for another 30 seconds.
- Add mint, almond, or vanilla essence for a unique flavor!

Nutrition Per Serving: Calories 37, Total Fat 2g, Protein 1g, Carbs 4g, Fiber 1.4g Cholesterol 0mg, Sodium 200mg, Potassium 272mg, Phosphorus 111mg

17. Italian Chicken Puree

Preparation time: 5 minutes | **Cooking time:** 1 minute | **Servings:** 1

Ingredients:

- 1 1/2 tablespoons of tomato sauce
- 1/8 teaspoon of pepper
- 1 teaspoon of Italian seasoning
- 1/4 cup of canned chicken
- 1/8 teaspoon of salt

Instructions:

- After blending with a small blender or the back of a spoon, the ingredients should be thoroughly combined and appear soft.
- Microwave for approximately 30 seconds and then serve.

Nutrition Per Serving: Calories 106, Total Fat 4g, Protein 13g, Carbs 3g, Fiber 1g Cholesterol 26mg, Sodium 656mg, Potassium 181mg, Phosphorus 62mg

18. Key Lime Tea

Preparation time: 5 minutes | **Cooking time:** 5 minutes | **Servings:** 2

Ingredients:

- 1 sprig of dill weed

- 1/16 teaspoon of cayenne pepper

- 2 cups of spring water

- 1 tablespoon of key lime juice

Instructions:

- A medium-sized saucepan should be filled with water and brought to boil over a medium-high flame.

- After 5 minutes of boiling, strain the tea into a bowl.

- Cayenne pepper is added after the lime juice has been thoroughly combined.

- Before serving, divide the tea between two mugs.

Nutrition Per Serving: Calories 2.4, Total Fat 0g, Protein 0g, Carbs 0.5g, Fiber 3g Cholesterol 5g, Sodium 90mg, Potassium 0mg, Phosphorus 0mg

19. Lime Black Bean Puree

Preparation time: 5 minutes | **Cooking time:** 20 minutes | **Servings:** 1

Ingredients:

- 1/4 cup of chicken or vegetable broth

- 1/2 tablespoon of juice from jarred jalapenos

- 1 tablespoon of protein powder unflavored

- 1/4 cup of rinsed black beans

- 1/2 tablespoon of lime juice

Instructions:

- Inside a small-sized saucepan, heat drained black beans over medium flame.

- Mix in the lime and jalapeno juices. Stir constantly while heating. At this point, add the chicken broth.

- After blending or mixing with a hand mixer, the components should be smooth. Put it in a dish.

- Allow it to cool slightly before mixing in the unflavored protein powder. Serve.

Nutrition Per Serving: Calories 94, Total Fat 1g, Protein 10g, Carbs 10g, Fiber 15g Cholesterol 0mg, Sodium 227mg, Potassium 611mg, Phosphorus 317mg

20. Mint Mojito

Preparation time: 5 minutes | **Cooking time:** 15 minutes | **Servings:** 1

Ingredients:

- 1/2 cup of any natural sweetener

- 2 tablespoons of lime juice (approx. 1/2 lime)

- 1/2 cup of fresh mint leaves

- 2 cups of water

Instructions:

- Bring water and natural sweetener to boil for about five minutes or till the mixture turns into syrup.

- For the mint mojito, place the mint leaves in a glass jar with a lid (such as a mason jar). Allow at least 20 minutes for the mint leaves to soak in the syrup. It can be used right away or saved for later.

- Ice should be poured halfway into a glass. Add one tablespoon of mint syrup and half a cup of cold water. After adding 2 tablespoons lime juice, stir well.

- To taste, add more mint syrup or lime juice.

Nutrition Per Serving: Calories 32, Total Fat 1g, Protein 1g, Carbs 3g, Fiber 0.4g Cholesterol 0mg, Sodium 3.4mg, Potassium 50mg, Phosphorus 23mg

21. Mango & Ginger Infused Water

Preparation time: 5 minutes | **Cooking time:** 0 minutes | **Servings:** 2

Ingredients:

- 1-inch of ginger, peeled and sliced

- 2 cups of ice

- 1 cup of diced mango

- Water, to top off

Instructions:

- Peel the ginger and cut it into 3-4 coin-sized slices.

- Pour the mango and ginger into a pitcher.

- Before adding water, place two cups of ice on top.

- Refrigerate for approximately 3 hours.

- Serve.

Nutrition Per Serving: Calories 1.3, Total Fat 0g, Protein 0g, Carbs 0.4g, Fiber 0.9g Cholesterol 0mg, Sodium 7.2mg, Potassium 74mg, Phosphorus 19mg

22. Nutty Creamy Wheat Bowl

Preparation time: 5 minutes | **Cooking time**: 10 minutes | **Servings**: 2

Ingredients:

- 1 tablespoon of uncooked Cream of Wheat
- Ground cinnamon and salt for seasoning
- 1 teaspoon of almond butter
- 4 ounces of nonfat milk
- ½ banana, mashed

Instructions:

- Inside a small-sized saucepan, combine the milk and Cream of Wheat. Cook the mixture in the saucepan over medium-high flame, stirring frequently to prevent lumps from forming.
- Simmer the cereal for 1 to 2 minutes on low heat, or till it thickens. Place the cereal in a bowl and season with salt to taste.
- Along with the almond butter, cinnamon is added. Top the cereal with mashed banana before serving.

Nutrition Per Serving: Calories 167, Total Fat 3g, Protein 10g, Carbs 26g, Fiber 2g Cholesterol 1mg, Sodium 100mg, Potassium 30mg, Phosphorus 10mg

23. Orange-Carrot Juice

Preparation time: 5 minutes | **Cooking time**: 15 minutes | **Servings**: 2

Ingredients:

- 1 medium-sized apple, cut into eighths
- 4 peeled large carrots
- 1 peeled and quartered medium orange
- 1 medium-sized yellow tomato, wedges
- Ice cubes

Instructions:

- Using a juicer, process the tomato, orange, apple, and carrots in this order, as directed by the manufacturer.

- Pour the juice into two glasses with ice if desired. Serve right away.

Nutrition Per Serving: Calories 111, Total Fat 1g, Protein 2g, Carbs 24g, Fiber 2g Cholesterol 0mg, Sodium 26mg, Potassium 496mg, Phosphorus 199mg

24. Orange Peach Iced Tea

Preparation time: 15 minutes | **Cooking time:** 0 minutes | **Servings:** 2

Ingredients:

- 2 cups of boiling water

- 1/2 large sliced fresh peach

- 1 tea bag

- 1/2 peeled and segmented clementine

- 1/2 tablespoon of sweetener

Instructions:

- In a pitcher, combine the peach, clementine, and sweetener. Before adding the water and tea bags, mash the fruit with a spoon. Refrigerate for one hour, or till completely cold. Using a slotted spoon, remove the fruit and tea bags.

Nutrition Per Serving: Calories 15, Total Fat 0g, Protein 0.1g, Carbs 3.7g, Fiber 0g Cholesterol 0mg, Sodium 15mg, Potassium 176mg, Phosphorus 43mg

25. Orange Vanilla Tea

Preparation time: 5 minutes | **Cooking time:** 10 minutes | **Servings:** 2

Ingredients:

- 0.25 teaspoon of vanilla

- 0.25 cup of water

- 2 sliced oranges

Instructions:

- Take out the pot and place it over a high flame. After adding the ingredients, allow this to come to boil.

- Remove the pot from the flame and set it aside to cool.

- When the mixture has cooled, drain it before serving.

Nutrition Per Serving: Calories 60, Total Fat 1g, Protein 2g, Carbs 14g, Fiber 1g Cholesterol 10mg, Sodium 100mg, Potassium 41mg, Phosphorus 32mg

26. PBJ Shake

Preparation time: 5 minutes | **Cooking time:** 0 minutes | **Servings:** 2

Ingredients:

- ½ cup of frozen strawberries or 5 to 6 fresh strawberries

- ½ cup of ice

- 1 small handful of baby spinach

- ½ cup of Greek yogurt

- ¼ cup of natural creamy peanut butter

Instructions:

- Inside a blender, combine all of the ingredients. Blend for approximately 2 minutes, or till completely smooth.

Nutrition Per Serving: Calories 554, Total Fat 41g, Protein 29g, Carbs 27g, Fiber 1g, Sugar 16g, Cholesterol 19mg, Sodium 30mg, Potassium 2mg, Phosphorus 2mg

27. Pureed Ricotta Broccoli

Preparation time: 5 minutes | **Cooking time:** 15 minutes | **Servings:** 4

Ingredients:

- 3 tablespoons of why protein isolate unflavored

- 1/2 cup of fat-free ricotta cheese

- 1 teaspoon of chopped Ginger

- 2 cloves of chopped garlic

- 2 cups of broccoli florets (fresh or frozen)

Instructions:

- Broccoli should be steamed till tender (around 10 to 15 minutes for fresh and 5 to 10 minutes for frozen).

- Pulse the remaining ingredients inside a food processor or blender till they reach the desired consistency.

- Season using salt and black pepper to taste.

Nutrition Per Serving: Calories 50, Total Fat 0g, Protein 7g, Carbs 5g, Fiber 1g, Cholesterol 0mg, Sodium 387mg, Potassium 80mg, Phosphorus 17mg

28. Protein Chocolate Pudding

Preparation time: 10 minutes | **Cooking time:** 0 minutes | **Servings:** 2

Ingredients:

- 1 cup of plain Greek yogurt with 0% fat

- 2 tablespoons of whey protein powder chocolate

Instructions:

- Combine all of the ingredients inside a bowl with a small rubber spatula and whisk them together till well combined.

Nutrition Per Serving: Calories 67, Total Fat 1g, Protein 13g, Carbs 4g, Fiber 0g Cholesterol 10mg, Sodium 132mg, Potassium 230mg, Phosphorus 93mg

29. Peppermint Tea

Preparation time: 1 minute | **Cooking time:** 5 minutes | **Servings:** 2

Ingredients:

- 4 cups of Hot water

- 5 cups of Peppermint leaf, dried

Instructions:

- Bring the water to boil inside a pot. After it begins to boil, add the peppermint leaves and turn off the flame completely.

- Allow the pot to cool for a few minutes after covering it.

- When the mixture has been strained and cooled, serve it.

Nutrition Per Serving: Calories 34.2, Total Fat 0g, Protein 0.1g, Carbs 9.1g, Fiber 0g Cholesterol 0mg, Sodium 2.4mg, Potassium 21mg, Phosphorus 11mg

30. Pureed Beans and Salsa

Preparation time: 10 minutes | **Cooking time**: 20 minutes | **Servings**: 2

Ingredients:

- 1 tablespoon of chicken broth

- 1/2 can of pinto beans (7 oz.)

- 1 tablespoon of salsa of your choice

- 1/2 scoop of whey protein powder unflavored

Instructions:

- Inside a pot, combine all of the ingredients. Place over a medium-high flame on the stovetop.

- Stir occasionally till the ingredients are thoroughly warmed. Combine all of the ingredients inside a blender.

- Blend at high speed for a few minutes or till the mixture appears smooth. Place in a serving bowl.

Nutrition Per Serving: Calories 128, Total Fat 1g, Protein 11g, Carbs 15g, Fiber 0.8g Cholesterol 0mg, Sodium 262mg, Potassium 378mg, Phosphorus 100mg

31. Peanut Butter Porridge

Preparation time: 5 minutes | **Cooking time**: 20 minutes | **Servings**: 1

Ingredients:

- 1/2 small chopped banana optional

- 1 tablespoon of natural peanut butter

- 1/4 cup of rolled oats

- 1/2 cup of low-fat milk

- 1 teaspoon of honey optional

Instructions:

- Inside a small-sized saucepan over medium-high flame, bring milk to simmer. After adding the oats and a pinch of salt, combine thoroughly. After bringing it to boil, reducing flame to medium, and simmering for 5 minutes, stir continuously with a wooden spoon till the porridge thickens.

- Combine the remaining ingredients with the peanut butter inside a mixing bowl. Combine the banana and honey, if using, in a mixing bowl.

Nutrition Per Serving: Calories 296, Total Fat 12g, Protein 11g, Carbs 40g, Fiber 4g Cholesterol 15mg, Sodium 117mg, Potassium 57.0 mg, Phosphorus 31mg

32. Pureed Salmon with Garlic and Lemon

Preparation time: 10 minutes | **Cooking time:** 0 minutes | **Servings:** 2

Ingredients:

- 2 tablespoons of low-fat mayonnaise

- 1/8 teaspoon of garlic powder

- 5 ounces of canned salmon

- 1 teaspoon of lemon juice

Instructions:

- Using a sieve, drain the water from the canned salmon.

- Salmon should be placed halfway inside a food processor.

- Add the lemon juice, mayonnaise, and garlic.

- Blend the mixture till it is smooth.

Nutrition Per Serving: Calories 88, Total Fat 4g, Protein 11g, Carbs 1g, Fiber 1g Cholesterol 15mg, Sodium 360mg, Potassium 442mg, Phosphorus 187mg

33. Pureed Tuna Salad

Preparation time: 10 minutes | **Cooking time**: 0 minutes | **Servings**: 2

Ingredients:

- 2 teaspoons of relish

- 1 (6 oz.) can of tuna packed in water

- 2 tablespoons of plain Greek yogurt

- 1 to 2 tablespoons of low-fat mayonnaise

- Salt & black pepper to taste

Instructions:

- A small food processor is used to combine tuna and relish.

- Using a food processor, shred the tuna.

- In a mixing bowl, combine the tuna relish and shredded tuna.

- Mayonnaise and yogurt should be mixed into the tuna mixture.

- To combine the ingredients, combine them all together.

- Season using salt and pepper as needed.

Nutrition Per Serving: Calories 78, Total Fat 3g, Protein 10g, Carbs 1.7g, Fiber 0.4g Cholesterol 27mg, Sodium 212mg, Potassium 365mg, Phosphorus 188mg

34. Pureed Celery Root

Preparation time: 5 minutes | **Cooking time**: 25 minutes | **Servings**: 6

Ingredients:

- 1 peeled large celery root and cut into chunks

- 2 tablespoons of butter

- 1/3 cup of heavy whipping cream

- 1 pinch of cayenne pepper

- Kosher salt to taste

- 1 lemon, juiced, divided

Instructions:

- Inside a saucepan, combine celery root, half of the lemon juice, and kosher salt, cover with water and bring to boil. Reduce the flame to medium-low and continue to cook for around 15 to 20 minutes or till the veggies are tender. Drain.

- Inside a blender, combine celery root, cream, and butter till smooth. Using a wooden spoon or spatula, push purée through a fine-mesh strainer into a bowl till completely smooth. Season using salt and cayenne pepper and drizzle with the remaining lemon juice.

Nutrition Per Serving: Calories 139, Total Fat 9.2g, Protein 2.5g, Carbs 14.7g, Fiber 2g, Cholesterol 0mg, Sodium 145mg, Potassium 600mg, Phosphorus 124mg

---

35. Parsnip Horsey Puree

Preparation time: 5 minutes | **Cooking time:** 25 minutes | **Servings:** 6

Ingredients:

- 2 peeled and cubed potatoes

- Salt and black pepper to taste

- 3 peeled and cubed parsnips

- 1/4 cup of evaporated milk fat-free

- 2 tablespoons of prepared horseradish

Instructions:

- Fill a large-sized saucepan halfway with salted water and add the parsnips and potatoes. Bring to boil over high flame, then reduce to a medium-low flame, cover, and cook for around 20 minutes or till vegetables are tender. Allow for a minute or two of steam drying after draining.

- Inside a food processor, combine the vegetables and process them till smooth. Season using salt and black pepper to taste after adding the milk and horseradish. Mix till everything is well combined.

Nutrition Per Serving: Calories 118, Total Fat 0.3g, Protein 3.1g, Carbs 26.8g, Fiber 6g, Cholesterol 0mg, Sodium 377mg, Potassium 565mg, Phosphorus 167mg

36. Rosemary Lemon Chicken

Preparation time: 5 minutes | **Cooking time:** 25 minutes | **Servings:** 2

Ingredients:

- 2 sprigs of fresh rosemary
- 1/2 lb. of boneless and skinless chicken thighs
- 1 minced or pressed clove of garlic
- 1/2 tablespoon of Dijon mustard
- 1 lemon- 1/2 juiced and zested & 1/2 sliced

Instructions:

- Preheat the oven at 425°F.
- Combine the lemon juice, lemon zest, mustard, and garlic inside a small-sized bowl, season using salt and pepper.
- Toss the chicken, rosemary, and lemon slices with the mustard mixture on a baking sheet with a rim.
- Place the lemons on top of the chicken in a single layer.
- Bake for around 20 to 25 minutes or till the internal temperature reaches 165°F.

Nutrition Per Serving: Calories 181, Total Fat 6g, Protein 31g, Carbs 2g, Fiber 6g Cholesterol 81mg, Sodium 570mg, Potassium 700mg, Phosphorus 363mg

37. Strawberry Ricotta Gelatin

Preparation time: 10 minutes | **Cooking time:** 0 minute | **Servings:** 4

Ingredients:

- 1 cup of cold water
- 1 package of strawberry gelatin sugar-free
- 2/3 cup of light ricotta cheese
- 1 cup of boiling water

Instructions:

- Fluff the ricotta cheese with a fork. Prepare four plates on which to pour the mixture.

- Inside a medium-sized mixing bowl, place the gelatin packet. Add 1 cup of boiling water and stir till completely dissolved. Incorporate the ricotta.

- Combine all of the ingredients inside a mixing bowl filled with cold water. Fill each of the four dishes halfway with the mixture. Refrigerate for at least 2 hours, or till completely set.

- Remove the gelatin top layer to reveal the thicker, darker-colored gelatin beneath.

Nutrition Per Serving: Calories 50, Total Fat 2g, Protein 5g, Carbs 1g, Fiber 0mg, Cholesterol 0mg, Sodium 296mg, Potassium 6mg, Phosphorus 0.1mg

38. Strawberry Greek Yogurt Whip

Preparation time: 10 minutes | **Cooking time:** 0 minutes | **Servings:** 2

Ingredients:

- 1/2 tablespoon of natural no-calorie sweetener

- 1/4 cup of plain Greek yogurt 0%

- 2 frozen strawberries

- 1/4 cup of light whipped topping

Instructions:

- Fill a small microwave-safe dish halfway with frozen strawberries. Defrost in the microwave for 60 seconds.

- Using kitchen shears, cut the strawberries inside the dish till they are slightly runny. Stir in the Greek yogurt.

- Stir in the sweetener. The Greek yogurt is finished by folding in the fluffy topping. Cover and chill the dish until ready to serve, or serve immediately. It can be eaten on its own or as a dip.

Nutrition Per Serving: Calories 24, Total Fat 1g, Protein 2g, Carbs 3g, Fiber 1g Cholesterol 6mg, Sodium 50mg, Potassium 198mg, Phosphorus 77mg

39. Tuna Salad Stuffed Tomatoes

Preparation time: 10 minutes | **Cooking time**: 0 minute | **Servings**: 2

Ingredients:

- 1 (4 oz.) can of tuna packed in water, drained

- 2 Roma tomatoes

- 1/4 teaspoon of each salt and pepper

- 1/8 teaspoon of curry powder

- 1/3 cup of fat-free Greek yogurt

Instructions:

- Cut the tomatoes in half and remove the seeds.

- Fill the tomatoes halfway with the remaining ingredients.

Nutrition Per Serving: Calories 105, Total Fat 0.1g, Protein 18g, Carbs 7g, Fiber 1g, Cholesterol 7mg, Sodium 208mg, Potassium 160mg, Phosphorus 78mg

40. Watermelon Juice

Preparation time: 5 minutes

Cooking time: 0 minutes

Servings: 2

Ingredients:

- 1 watermelon, peeled, deseeded, cubed

- 2 cups of coconut water

- 1 tablespoon of date sugar

- ½ of key lime, juiced, zest

Instructions:

- Combine the watermelon pieces, lime zest, juice, and date sugar inside a high-speed food processor or blender. Blend or process till smooth.

- Fill two tall glasses two-thirds full with the watermelon mixture, then top with coconut water.

- Mix everything together before serving.

Nutrition Per Serving: Calories 1.3, Total Fat 0.9g, Protein 9.9g, Carbs 7g, Fiber 0.4g Cholesterol 0mg, Sodium 19mg, Potassium 106mg, Phosphorus 78mg

Chapter 5: Breakfast Recipes

1. BLT Romaine Boat

Preparation time: 10 minutes | **Cooking time:** 0 minute | **Servings:** 1

Ingredients:

- 2 slices of cooked bacon

- 1 Romaine lettuce leaf

- 3 slices of tomato

- Black pepper

- 1 hard-boiled egg

Instructions:

- Put everything in a romaine lettuce leaf and eat!

Nutrition Per Serving: Calories 150, Total Fat 10g, Protein 12g, Carbs 5g, Fiber 4.8g, Cholesterol 0mg, Sodium 188mg, Potassium 566mg, Phosphorus 47mg

2. Breakfast Avocado Toast

Preparation time: 5 minutes | **Cooking time:** 0 minute | **Servings:** 2

Ingredients:

- 2 slices of whole-wheat toast

- 1 lime juiced

- 2 poached eggs

- Salt and black pepper

- 1 avocado sliced

Instructions:

- The bread should be toasted.

- Using a knife, cut the avocado into thin strips.

- Season the avocado using salt, black pepper, and lime juice before serving.

- On top, place a poached or cooked egg.

Nutrition Per Serving: Calories 269, Total Fat 16g, Protein 12g, Carbs 12g, Fiber 5g, Cholesterol 0mg, Sodium 439mg, Potassium 381mg, Phosphorus 157mg

---

3. Breakfast Coffee Rubbed Steak

Preparation time: 5 minutes | **Cooking time:** 15 minutes | **Servings:** 4

Ingredients:

- 1 lb. of lean sirloin steak

- 2 teaspoons of cinnamon

- 1 tablespoon of ground coffee

- Pinch of black pepper and salt

- 1 tablespoon of chili powder

Instructions:

- Season the meat on both sides using salt. Spices should be combined inside a small-sized mixing bowl. The meat should be seasoned on both sides.

- Preheat a large-sized skillet over high flame. Sear the steak on both sides till done to your liking (around 3 to 5 minutes on each side for medium-rare).

- Set aside for 5 minutes on a chopping board. (Now would be a good time to make some scrambled eggs to go with it!) Serve thinly sliced against the grain.

Nutrition Per Serving: Calories 153, Total Fat 5g, Protein 25g, Carbs 2g, Fiber 3g, Cholesterol 14mg, Sodium 490mg, Potassium 234mg, Phosphorus 78mg

4. Berries with Cottage Cheese

Preparation time: 5 minutes | **Cooking time:** 0 minute | **Servings:** 1

Ingredients:

- 1/3 cup of strawberries, raspberries or blueberries

- 2/3 cup of 2% cottage cheese

Instructions:

- Combine all of the ingredients, then serve and enjoy!

Nutrition Per Serving: Calories 120, Total Fat 3g, Protein 21g, Carbs 8g, Fiber 0g, Cholesterol 14mg, Sodium 348mg, Potassium 141mg, Phosphorus 34mg

5. Cherry Avocado Smoothie

Preparation time: 5 minutes | **Cooking time:** 0 minutes | **Servings:** 2

Ingredients:

- 1 cup of fresh cherries

- 1 cup of coconut water, sugar-free

- ½ ripe avocado, chopped

- 1 whole lime

Instructions:

- After peeling the avocado, cut it in half. Remove the pit and chop it into bite-sized chunks. Refrigerate any leftovers for later use. Set aside.

- Rinse the cherries inside a large colander under cold running water. Before cutting each in half, remove the pits. Set aside.

- The lime must be peeled and cut in half. Set aside.

- Now, combine the avocado, coconut water, cherries, and lime juice. After pulsing to combine, transfer to a serving glass.

- Place in the refrigerator for 10 minutes before serving with a few ice cubes.

Nutrition Per Serving: Calories 128, Total Fat 7g, Protein 1g, Carbs 17g, Fiber 3g Cholesterol 0mg, Sodium 30mg, Potassium 107mg, Phosphorus 14mg

6. Creamy Banana Protein Shake

Preparation time: 5 minutes | **Cooking time:** 0 minute | **Servings:** 1 shake

Ingredients:

- 1 scoop of vanilla whey protein powder

- 1/2 teaspoon of banana extract

- 8 oz. of unsweetened almond milk

- 1/4 teaspoon of vanilla extract

Instructions:

- Shake the ingredients together in a shaker cup vigorously. Pour over ice and serve.

- To make it creamier, combine the ingredients in a blender with 1/2 cup of ice and 1/4 cup of low-fat cottage cheese. Blend on high speed till completely smooth.

Nutrition Per Serving: Calories 143, Total Fat 5g, Protein 21g, Carbs 4g, Fiber 1.2g, Cholesterol 12mg, Sodium 212mg, Potassium 528mg, Phosphorus 127mg

7. Chicken Sausage and Pineapple Skewers

Preparation time: 5 minutes | **Cooking time:** 10 minutes | **Servings:** 4

Ingredients:

- 1 cup of fresh pineapple chunks

- 4 links of chicken sausage pre-cooked

Instructions:

- Preheat the grill at medium-high.

- Cut the links of chicken sausage into 1-inch pieces. If you haven't already done so, slice the pineapple now. Thread two chicken sausages onto skewers for each pineapple piece.

- Grill for around 4 minutes on each side. Take the skewers off the grill and serve right away.

- Another possibility is to brush the skewers with a low-sugar barbecue sauce before cooking.

Nutrition Per Serving: Calories 101, Total Fat 2.5g, Protein 13g, Carbs 6g, Fiber 1g, Cholesterol 30mg, Sodium 320mg, Potassium 147mg, Phosphorus 28mg

8. Cinnamon Protein Shake

Preparation time: 5 minutes | **Cooking time:** 0 minute | **Servings:** 1

Ingredients:

- 1 cup of unsweetened almond milk

- 1/2 teaspoon of cinnamon

- 1 stick scoop of vanilla protein powder

- 1/2 teaspoon of vanilla extract

- 1 packet of Splenda

Instructions:

- Inside a blender, combine all of the ingredients and blend till smooth.

- Sprinkle with cinnamon as a finishing touch!

Nutrition Per Serving: Calories 201, Total Fat 3g, Protein 30g, Carbs 7g, Fiber 1.2g, Cholesterol 12mg, Sodium 212mg, Potassium 528mg, Phosphorus 165mg

9. Chocolate Protein Mocha Frappuccino

Preparation time: 10 minutes | **Cooking time:** 0 minute | **Servings:** 1

Ingredients:

- 1 teaspoon of sugar-free coffee flavoring

- 10 ice cubes

- 1/2 cup of almond milk

- 1 cup of cold coffee

- 1 scoop of chocolate protein powder

Instructions:

- Inside a blender, combine all of the ingredients and serve!

Nutrition Per Serving: Calories 195, Total Fat 3g, Protein 30g, Carbs 10.5g, Fiber 4g, Cholesterol 40mg, Sodium 350mg, Potassium 202mg, Phosphorus 23mg

10. Egg and Zucchini Cups

Preparation time: 5 minutes | **Cooking time:** 20 minutes | **Servings:** 6

Ingredients:

- 2 oz. of diced ham

- 2 oz. of shredded cheddar cheese

- 9 eggs

- Salt and pepper to taste

- 2 zucchinis

Instructions:

- Using a mandolin slicer, cut your zucchini into strips or super skinny circles.

- Line each muffin tin with thin layers of zucchini using a large muffin tin.

- Each one should be stuffed with ham and cheese.

- Whisk the eggs thoroughly with salt and black pepper.

- Spoon the eggs into the muffin cups and bake for around 20 to 22 minutes or till done.

Nutrition Per Serving: Calories 166, Total Fat 11g, Protein 14g, Carbs 1g, Fiber 6g, Cholesterol 35mg, Sodium 690mg, Potassium 324mg, Phosphorus 101mg

11. Egg and Tomato Scrambler

Preparation time: 5 minutes | **Cooking time:** 15 minutes | **Servings:** 4

Ingredients:

- 5 eggs

- 1/4 cup of 2% shredded cheddar cheese

- 4 strips of turkey bacon

- 1/2 cup of chopped red bell pepper

- 3/4 cup of cherry tomatoes

Instructions:

- Cook the turkey bacon till crispy on both sides in a pan coated using cooking spray over medium-high flame.

- Cool the turkey bacon on a cutting board. Toss the bell pepper and cherry tomatoes together in a pan, tossing frequently. In the meantime, chop the turkey bacon into small pieces.

- When the cherry tomatoes start to "blister," whip the eggs with a fork and add to the skillet. Constantly whisk with a fork to scramble eggs and combine ingredients. Add the cheese and turkey bacon. Serve immediately.

Nutrition Per Serving: Calories 150, Total Fat 10g, Protein 12g, Carbs 3g, Fiber 1g, Cholesterol 56mg, Sodium 420mg, Potassium 145mg, Phosphorus 21mg

12. Enchilada Flavored Eggs

Preparation time: 5 minutes | **Cooking time:** 10 minutes | **Servings:** 4

Ingredients:

- 4 eggs

- 10 oz. enchilada sauce

- Pinch of salt

Instructions:

- Heat the enchilada sauce inside a medium-sized saucepan till it begins to simmer.

- Make a well in the sauce for each egg using a spoon. Rep by nestling another cracked egg in the sauce. Cover for 5 minutes for soft yolks and 7 minutes for hard yolks.

- Transfer the eggs to serving dishes and drizzle with a little sauce.

Nutrition Per Serving: Calories 90, Total Fat 5g, Protein 6g, Carbs 4g, Fiber 0g, Cholesterol 15mg, Sodium 240mg, Potassium 101mg, Phosphorus 23mg

13. Gruyere Bacon Egg Bites

Preparation time: 5 minutes | **Cooking time**: 25 minutes | **Servings**: 12

Ingredients:

- 1 cup of grated gruyere cheese

- 8 slices of cooked bacon

- Salt and black pepper

- 2 teaspoons of sour cream

- 10 eggs

Instructions:

- Combine the eggs, cheese, salt, sour cream, and pepper inside a large-sized mixing bowl.

- To make the eggs fluffy, whisk them till they are light and fluffy.

- Set aside a muffin pan that has been sprayed using cooking spray.

- Preheat the oven at 300 degrees F.

- Each slice of bacon should be cut into three smaller pieces. Make an X with two pieces in each egg cup.

- Bake the egg cups till they are firm (it will take around 20 minutes).

Nutrition Per Serving: Calories 110, Total Fat 8g, Protein 9g, Carbs 0g. Fiber 2g, Cholesterol 43mg, Sodium 752mg, Potassium 345mg, Phosphorus 98mg

14. High-Protein Pancakes

Preparation time: 5 minutes | **Cooking time:** 10 minutes | **Servings:** 2

Ingredients:

- 1 cup of low-fat cottage cheese

- 1/3 cup of whole-wheat pastry flour

- Nonstick cooking spray

- 3 eggs

- 1½ tablespoons of coconut oil, melted

Instructions:

- Inside a large-sized mixing bowl, lightly whisk the eggs.

- Simply whisk in the flour, cottage cheese, and coconut oil to combine.

- Before heating a large-sized skillet or griddle, spray it lightly using cooking spray.

- Using a measuring cup, pour 1/3 cup of batter per pancake into the skillet. Cook each pancake for around 2 to 3 minutes or till bubbles appear all over the surface. Flip the pancakes over and cook for another 1 to 2 minutes, or till golden brown.

- Serve immediately.

- On top, drizzle with plain yogurt, unsweetened applesauce, fresh berries, or sugar-free syrup. You can also try them with bananas and natural peanut butter on a regular basis.

Nutrition Per Serving: Calories 182, Total Fat 10g, Protein 12g, Carbs 10g, Fiber 0.5g Cholesterol 4mg, Sodium 89mg, Potassium 70mg, Phosphorus 23mg

15. Italian-Style Poached Eggs

Preparation time: 5 minutes | **Cooking time:** 20 minutes | **Servings:** 4

Ingredients:

- 4 leaves of fresh basil, break into small pieces

- 3 to 4 pieces of sliced jarred roasted red pepper

- 4 eggs

- Pinch of salt and black pepper

- 16 oz. of low-sugar marinara sauce

Instructions:

- Preheat a large-sized rimmed skillet on medium-high flame.

- Add the marinara sauce and the chopped red peppers.

- With the back of a spoon, make a "well" and place one egg inside. Rep with the remaining three eggs.

- Season to taste using salt and pepper.

- Cook for 12 minutes or till the eggs are hard when shaken in the pan.

- Remove from the flame and toss with the shredded basil before serving on a platter or in a bowl.

Nutrition Per Serving: Calories 114, Total Fat 6g, Protein 8g, Carbs 4g, Fiber 0g, Cholesterol 18mg, Sodium 149mg, Potassium 69mg, Phosphorus 0mg

16. Magical Egg Muffins

Preparation time: 5 minutes | **Cooking time:** 20 minutes | **Servings:** 6

Ingredients:

- 1/2 cup of cooked and chopped spinach

- 1/4 cup of grated cheddar cheese

- 6 eggs

- 1/2 cup of chopped ham or cooked middle bacon

Instructions:

- Preheat the oven at 180°F.

- Spray a muffin pan using cooking oil spray to make 6 cups.

- Inside a large-sized mixing bowl, whisk the eggs till the yolk and white are well combined. Mix in the spinach, ham or bacon, and cheese till thoroughly combined.

- Bake for around 15 to 18 minutes, or till the eggs are set, after evenly dividing the egg mixture among the muffin cups.

Nutrition Per Serving: Calories 95, Total Fat 7g, Protein 7g, Carbs 1g, Fiber 2g, Cholesterol 79mg, Sodium 577mg, Potassium 218mg, Phosphorus 67mg

17. Mozzarella and Spinach Egg Casserole

Preparation time: 5 minutes | **Cooking time:** 25 minutes | **Servings:** 6

Ingredients:

- 10 oz. of frozen spinach thawed & squeezed dry

- 1 cup of shredded low-fat mozzarella cheese

- 2 cloves of minced garlic and pinch of seasoning salt

- 1/3 cup of sliced green onion

- 12 eggs

Instructions:

- Preheat the oven at 375 degrees F. Spray an 8.5 x 12-inch casserole dish using nonstick cooking spray.

- Cover the bottom of the dish with spinach. On top, sprinkle with garlic, cheese, and green onions.

- Inside a separate dish, whisk the eggs and season using salt. Over the spinach mixture, pour the eggs. Whisk the eggs and spinach mixture together till well combined and evenly distributed in the bottom of the dish.

- Bake for approximately 20 minutes or till the mixture is firm. Allow to cool for 5 minutes before slicing. It goes well with a dash of Tabasco.

Nutrition Per Serving: Calories 201, Total Fat 13g, Protein 18g, Carbs 2g, Fiber 0.5g, Cholesterol 21mg, Sodium 423mg, Potassium 287mg, Phosphorus 47mg

18. Protein Pumpkin Latte

Preparation time: 10 minutes | **Cooking time:** 5 minutes | **Servings:** 1

Ingredients:

- 1 scoop of vanilla protein powder
- 2 almond milk creamer
- 8 oz. of freshly brewed coffee
- Whip cream for garnishing
- 1 oz. of pumpkin puree

Instructions:

- Make some coffee.
- Whisk together the creamer, protein, and pumpkin inside a cup till it resembles pudding. Continue whisking till no lumps remain.
- Then, slowly pour in the coffee while constantly swirling.
- Finish with a cinnamon sprinkling and a dollop of whipped cream.

Nutrition Per Serving: Calories 202, Total Fat 5g, Protein 25g, Carbs 13g, Fiber 1g, Cholesterol 35mg, Sodium 206mg, Potassium 146mg, Phosphorus 34mg

19. Protein Hot Chocolate

Preparation time: 10 minutes | **Cooking time:** 0 minute | **Servings:** 1

Ingredients:

- 8 boiling water
- 1 scoop of chocolate protein powder
- 2 oz. of almond milk

Instructions:

- In the bottom of your mug, combine your powder and almond milk and thoroughly stir.
- Stir till the mixture resembles pudding and there are no lumps.

- Slowly pour in your water, swirling constantly. This must take at least 2 minutes to complete! This will produce a rich, creamy hot chocolate that is free of lumps.

- Top with whipped cream and a dusting of chocolate powder!

Nutrition Per Serving: Calories 85, Total Fat 2g, Protein 22g, Carbs 4g, Fiber 1.4g, Cholesterol 0mg, Sodium 200mg, Potassium 179mg, Phosphorus 52mg

20. Swiss and Mushroom Egg Cups

Preparation time: 5 minutes | **Cooking time:** 25 minutes | **Servings:** 6

Ingredients:

- 1 cup of chopped mushrooms

- 1/2 cup of 2% cottage cheese

- 1 cup of chopped ham

- 1 cup of grated low-fat Swiss cheese

- 12 eggs

Instructions:

- Preheat the oven at 350 degrees F.

- Inside a large-sized mixing bowl, crack the eggs. Whisk the yolks till they are broken down.

- With the egg, combine the remaining ingredients.

- A 12-cup muffin pan is sprayed using nonstick cooking spray. Fill two-thirds of the way with the egg mixture.

- Bake for around 20 to 25 minutes, then remove from the oven and allow to cool before serving. It reheats well as well!

Nutrition Per Serving: Calories 277, Total Fat 18g, Protein 24g, Carbs 5g, Fiber 1g, Cholesterol 43mg, Sodium 440mg, Potassium 220mg, Phosphorus 34mg

Chapter 6: Sides and Snacks

1. Asian Green Beans Roasted

Preparation time: 5 minutes | **Cooking time:** 15 minutes | **Servings:** 2

Ingredients:

- 1 teaspoon of Olive oil extra-virgin

- 8 oz. of fresh green beans

- 1 tablespoon of tamari

Instructions:

- After removing the ends, cut the green beans in half.

- Put the green beans in a re-sealable plastic bag or a container with a lid. Shake vigorously to combine the tamari and olive oil.

- Fill the air fryer basket halfway with green beans. Cook for about 10 minutes at 390°F, tossing halfway through.

Nutrition Per Serving: Calories 58, Fat 2g, Carbohydrates 8g, Protein 3g, Fiber 1g, Cholesterol 2mg, Sodium 110mg, Potassium 345mg, Phosphorus 72mg

2. Apple Chips

Preparation time: 5 minutes | **Cooking time:** 25 minutes | **Servings:** 4

Ingredients:

- ½ teaspoon of ground cinnamon

- 2 cored and thinly sliced apples

- 1 ½ teaspoons of honey

Instructions:

- Preheat the oven at 390 degrees F.

- Arrange apple slices on a baking sheet.

- Combine honey and cinnamon in a dish, spread over apple slices.

- Bake for about 20 minutes, or till the apples are dry and the edges curl. Transfer the apple chips to a wire rack to cool and crisp.

Nutrition Per Serving: Calories 24, Fat 0.1g, Carbohydrates 7g, Protein 0.1g, Fiber 1g, Cholesterol 0mg, Sodium 1mg, Potassium 35mg, Phosphorus 2mg

3. Bacon Wrapped Honey Mustard Bites

Preparation time: 5 minutes | **Cooking time:** 15 minutes | **Servings:** 6 halves

Ingredients:

- 1 lb. of boneless and skinless chicken breast

- 2 tablespoons of honey mustard (mustard not dressing)

- 10 strips of turkey bacon

Instructions:

- Chicken should be cut into 1-inch-long pieces. Transfer to a mixing bowl and combine with 1 tablespoon of honey mustard.

- Cut turkey bacon strips in half and wrap the chicken in them. Use a toothpick to secure it.

- After preheating the oven at 425°F, bake for about 10 minutes. Remove from the oven and sprinkle a pinch of mustard on top of each bite. Cook for another 5 minutes in the oven. Remove the food from the oven, set it aside to cool, and serve.

Nutrition Per Serving: Calories 128, Total Fat 4g, Protein 19g, Carbs 1g, Fiber 0g, Cholesterol 24mg, Sodium 660mg, Potassium 341mg, Phosphorus 76mg

4. Butternut Squash Fries

Preparation time: 10 minutes | **Cooking time:** 15 minutes | **Servings:** 4

Ingredients:

- 1/2 teaspoon of Cajun seasoning, or to taste

- 1 pound of butternut squash - peeled, seeded, & cut into thick French fries

- 1 pinch of salt to taste

- Cooking spray

- 1/4 teaspoon of ground black pepper, or to taste

Instructions:

- Preheat the oven at 450°F. Coat a baking sheet using cooking spray.

- Before placing the butternut squash fries on the coated baking sheet, absorb any excess moisture with paper towels. Season using salt, black pepper, and Cajun seasoning to taste.

- In a preheated oven, bake for around 15 to 20 minutes, rotating once, till gently brown and tender.

Nutrition Per Serving: Calories 52, Total fat 0.1g, Protein 1.2g, Carbs 13.5g, Fiber 6g, Cholesterol 0mg, Sodium 172mg, Potassium 596mg, Phosphorus 134mg

5. Cheesy Asparagus Fries

Preparation time: 10 minutes | **Cooking time:** 20 minutes | **Servings:** 2

Ingredients:

- 1/2 lb. of asparagus spears

- 1 tablespoon of light mayo

- 1/4 cup of grated parmesan cheese

- 1 1/2 large egg whites

- 1 tablespoon of dried thyme

Instructions:

- Preheat the oven at 375°F. The stalks of asparagus should be removed.

- Combine egg whites and light mayonnaise inside a mixing bowl. Whisk everything together till it's completely smooth.

- Combine dried thyme and grated parmesan cheese inside a mixing bowl.

- Each asparagus spear must be dipped in the egg-white mixture before being pressed into the cheese mixture. After applying the cheese, place it on a baking sheet lined with foil or a baking stone.

- Bake for about 20 minutes after all of the spears have been lined up on the baking sheet. Remove the dish from the oven and serve.

Nutrition Per Serving: Calories 141, Total Fat 6g, Protein 17g, Carbs 5g, Fiber 2g Cholesterol 0mg, Sodium 180mg, Potassium 157mg, Phosphorus 13mg

6. Chocolate Energy Balls

Preparation time: 10 minutes | **Cooking time:** 0 minutes | **Servings:** 4

Ingredients:

- 1 cup of raw hemp seeds

- 6 pitted Medjool dates

- ⅓ cup of cocoa powder

Instructions:

- Grind hemp seeds to a powder inside a food processor, add dates and cocoa powder and process till smooth. Roll the dough into a tight ball to make it into balls.

Nutrition Per Serving: Calories 184, Fat 12.4g, Carbohydrates 12g, Protein 9.3g, Fiber 2g, Cholesterol 0mg, Sodium 1.2mg, Potassium 127.3mg, Phosphorus 27.4mg

7. Cauliflower Rice

Preparation time: 5 minutes | **Cooking time:** 10 minutes | **Servings:** 2

Ingredients:

- 1 teaspoon of extra-virgin olive oil
- 1 cauliflower head

Instructions:

- To prepare the cauliflower, remove the leaves and stems from the head. Divide it into four equal parts.
- Process the cauliflower inside a food processor till it is reduced to rice-sized pieces. Any remaining stem fragments may need to be removed. You could also use a box grater to grate the cauliflower.
- The riced cauliflower should be transferred to a plate or bowl and dried using a paper towel.
- A small skillet with olive oil is heated over a medium flame. Pour the cauliflower into the hot oil. Sauté for 5 to 6 minutes or till tender. Cauliflower rice can also be steamed, but any excess liquid should be drained before serving.

Nutrition Per Serving: Calories 12, Total Fat 0g, Protein 1g, Carbs 2g, Fiber 2g Cholesterol 0mg, Sodium 30mg, Potassium 299mg, Phosphorus 58mg

8. Caprese Salad

Preparation time: 10 minutes | **Cooking time:** 0 minutes | **Servings:** 2

Ingredients:

- 1/2 cup of cherry tomatoes
- 1/4 cup of balsamic dressing
- 1/2 red onion
- 4 tablespoons of fresh mozzarella
- 3 tablespoons of fresh basil

Instructions:

- Cheese cubes can be made by dicing them.
- Cut the tomatoes into bite-sized pieces.

- Red onions should be thinly sliced.

- Basil should be powdered to a fine powder.

- Combine all of the ingredients inside a mixing bowl. To taste, add the dressing and sprinkle of black pepper.

Nutrition Per Serving: Calories 167, Total Fat 12g, Protein 10g, Carbs 5g, Fiber 1g Cholesterol 44mg, Sodium 439mg, Potassium 254mg, Phosphorus 76mg

---

9. Crispy Baked Sweet Potato Fries

Preparation time: 5 minutes | **Cooking time:** 20 minutes | **Servings:** 2)

Ingredients:

- 1 large-sized sweet potato

- 2 teaspoons of extra virgin olive oil

- Fine sea salt & freshly ground black pepper to season

Instructions:

- Preheat the oven at 400°F.

- Peel and cut the sweet potato into fries-like shapes.

- Place the fries on a baking sheet.

- Drizzle with olive oil and season using salt & black pepper.

- Shake the fries in the baking pan to coat them with the olive oil.

- After that, season the fries and distribute them evenly across the tray.

- Bake for about 10 minutes on one side, then flip and bake for another 10 minutes. If they start to brown too quickly, remove them from the oven.

Nutrition Per Serving: Calories 235, Total fat 14.2g, Protein 2.1g, Carbs 26.8g, Fiber 2g, Cholesterol 0mg, Sodium 104mg, Potassium 119mg, Phosphorus 23mg

10. Easy and Quick Lima Beans

Preparation time: 5 minutes | **Cooking time:** 25 minutes | **Servings:** 6

Ingredients:

- 1 (16 ounces) package of baby lima beans frozen

- 1 1/2 cups of chicken broth

- Cooking spray

- 1/2 finely chopped medium-sized onion

Instructions:

- Coat a large-sized pot using cooking spray and heat on medium. Inside a skillet, cook onions till tender and transparent. Bring the chicken broth to boil. Add just enough water to cover the lima beans. Bring to a boil, then reduce to a low flame, cover, and cook for around 20 minutes or till the beans are tender.

Nutrition Per Serving: Calories 84, Total fat 0.1g, Protein 4.1g, Carbs 15.9g, Fiber 14g, Cholesterol 0mg, Sodium 143mg, Potassium 755mg, Phosphorus 126mg

11. Feta Cucumber Rolls

Preparation time: 10 minutes | **Cooking time:** 0 minute | **Servings:** 4

Ingredients:

- 4 oz. of reduced-fat feta crumbles

- 1 teaspoon of dried oregano

- 2 tablespoons of plain Greek yogurt

- 1 large cucumber

- 1 tablespoon of sun-dried tomato pesto

Instructions:

- Cut the cucumber into thin slices using a mandolin or a simple slicer.

- Inside a mixing bowl, combine the remaining ingredients, pressing the crumbled feta into the mixture with the back of a spoon.

- Fill each cucumber slice with about a teaspoon of the mixture, roll it up, and secure it with a toothpick.

Nutrition Per Serving: Calories 36, Total Fat 2g, Protein 3g, Carbs 2g, Fiber 1g, Cholesterol 0g, Sodium 30mg, Potassium 149mg, Phosphorus 37mg

12. Feta Stuffed Watermelon Blocks

Preparation time: 5 minutes | **Cooking time:** 0 minute | **Servings:** 4

Ingredients:

- 2 oz. of low-fat feta cheese crumbles
- 4 (1 oz.) blocks of seedless watermelon
- 2 tablespoons of chopped fresh basil
- Balsamic vinegar for drizzling

Instructions:

- Watermelon should be cut into squares. A small portion of the middle should be removed.
- Place crumbled feta in the center.
- Add the basil leaves (and balsamic vinegar if liked).

Nutrition Per Serving: Calories 50, Total Fat 2g, Protein 4g, Carbs 3g, Fiber 1g, Cholesterol 0mg, Sodium 20mg, Potassium 80mg, Phosphorus 14mg

13. Garlic Snow Peas and Mushrooms

Preparation time: 10 minutes | **Cooking time:** 10 minutes | **Servings:** 4

Ingredients:

- 2 minced cloves of garlic
- 3 cups of snow peas
- 1 cup of sliced baby mushrooms
- 2 tablespoons of chicken broth
- 1 tablespoon of low-fat margarine

Instructions:

- Peas should be rinsed and dried. Pull the strings and break off the pea tips.

- Melt butter inside a nonstick skillet over medium-high flame. Pour in the peas, mushrooms, and broth. Cook, stirring occasionally, for 3-4 minutes or till the broth has evaporated and the vegetables are crisp and tender.

- Stir in the garlic and continue to cook for another minute or till fragrant.

Nutrition Per Serving: Calories 63, Fat 3g, Carbohydrates 7g, Protein 3g, Fiber 2g, Cholesterol 8mg, Sodium 57mg, Potassium 240mg, Phosphorus 37mg

14. Grilled Creamy Parmesan Tomatoes

Preparation time: 5 minutes | **Cooking time:** 15 minutes | **Servings:** 6 halves

Ingredients:

- 1/4 cup of reduced-fat grated parmesan cheese

- 1/4 teaspoon of dried oregano

- 3 Roma tomatoes

- 1/2 cup of plain 0% fat Greek yogurt

- 1/4 teaspoon of dried basil

Instructions:

- Cut tomatoes in half lengthwise. Remove the seeds and discard them.

- Fill each tomato half almost to the brim with Greek yogurt.

- Fill with the Parmesan cheese and herbs on top.

- Broil for around 10 to 12 minutes or till the skin begins to blister.

Nutrition Per Serving: Calories 30, Total Fat 1g, Protein 3g, Carbs 3g, Fiber 2g, Cholesterol 0mg, Sodium 225mg, Potassium 355mg, Phosphorus 107mg

15. Honey Oat and Peanut Butter Balls

Preparation time: 10 minutes | **Cooking time:** 0 minute | **Servings:** 20 balls

Ingredients:

- 3 tablespoons of honey

- 1.5 cups of dark chocolate chips

- 2 cups of rolled oats

- 1 cup of almond meal

- 1.33 cups of smooth, natural peanut butter

Instructions:

- Inside a mixing bowl, combine all of the ingredients.

- Make a ball with a tablespoon of the mixture, or press it into a pan lined using baking paper and cut it into squares. Any leftovers should be refrigerated.

Nutrition Per Serving: Calories 208, Total Fat 14g, Protein 7g, Carbs 16g, Fiber 2g, Cholesterol 0mg, Sodium 28mg, Potassium 0mg, Phosphorus 0mg

16. Orange Infused Green Beans

Preparation time: 5 minutes | **Cooking time:** 15 minutes | **Servings:** 4

Ingredients:

- 1 lb. of fresh green beans
- 1/4 teaspoon of sea salt
- 1 small orange
- 1/4 teaspoon of black pepper

Instructions:

- Green beans should be rinsed after breaking off the ends. Allow it to dry naturally. Peel and cut the orange into long strips.
- Bring a medium pot half-full of water to boil. Add the green beans and orange peel at this point. Bring to boil and cook for about 7-8 minutes.
- After draining the green beans, season using salt and black pepper. Sprinkle a small amount of fresh orange juice over the beans to combine the flavors. Combine with a lean protein.

Nutrition Per Serving: Calories 40, Total Fat 0.1g, Protein 2g, Carbs 7g, Fiber 2.6g, Cholesterol 0g, Sodium 311mg, Potassium 130mg, Phosphorus 54mg

17. Pan-Fried Sprouts with Nutmeg

Preparation time: 5 minutes | **Cooking time:** 15 minutes | **Servings:** 6

Ingredients:

- 1/4 teaspoon of ground nutmeg
- Salt & pepper to season
- 600g of Brussels sprouts
- 40g of butter

Instructions:

- After slicing the sprouts in half, parboil them in hot water for about 4 minutes.
- Parboiling is the process of cooking food in boiling water till it softens, then removing it before it is fully cooked.

- Melt the butter in a wok over high flame, then add the sprouts and stir-fry for 4 minutes.

- Season using salt and black pepper, then sprinkle with nutmeg before serving!

Nutrition Per Serving: Calories 84, Total fat 5.9g, Protein 2.6g, Carbs 7.1g, Fiber 4g, Cholesterol 0mg, Sodium 135mg, Potassium 533mg, Phosphorus 55mg

18. Parmesan Zucchini Chips

Preparation time: 5 minutes | **Cooking time:** 25 minutes | **Servings:** 4

Ingredients:

- 1 cup of reduced-fat grated parmesan cheese

- 1/4 teaspoon of each salt and pepper

- 2 beaten eggs

- 1 large zucchini

Instructions:

- Preheat the oven at 425°F.

- Wash the zucchini and cut it into thin slices.

- Inside a small-sized mixing bowl, combine the eggs. First, roll the zucchini slices in parmesan cheese.

- Roll the Parmesan cheese slices in the egg.

- Cover a cookie sheet using foil or a baking stone. Distribute the zucchini slices evenly.

- Season using salt & pepper to taste.

- Bake for around 10-12 minutes on one side before flipping and baking for another 10-12 minutes on the other.

Nutrition Per Serving: Calories 131, Total Fat 5g, Protein 9g, Carbs 7g, Fiber 2.6g, Cholesterol 11mg, Sodium 487mg, Potassium 561mg, Phosphorus 100mg

19. Roasted Parmesan Artichoke

Preparation time: 5 minutes | **Cooking time:** 25 minutes | **Servings:** 4

Ingredients:

- 1/2 cup of shredded parmesan cheese

- 3 minced or pressed cloves of garlic

- 1 (12 oz.) jar of Artichoke heart quarters, drained

- 5 sprays of olive oil spray

Instructions:

- Preheat the oven at 425°F.

- Place the artichoke hearts inside a shallow baking dish and drain them.

- Inside a small-sized mixing bowl, combine the remaining ingredients. Place the artichokes on top of the mixture.

- Bake for around 20 to 25 minutes. Allow it to cool for 5-10 minutes before serving.

Nutrition Per Serving: Calories 80, Total Fat 4g, Protein 5g, Carbs 5g, Fiber 0g, Cholesterol 15mg, Sodium 135mg, Potassium 67mg, Phosphorus 11mg

20. Roasted Chickpeas

Preparation time: 5 minutes | **Cooking time:** 25 minutes | **Servings:** 4

Ingredients:

- 2 tablespoons of olive oil

- ½ pound of dried chickpeas

- A pinch of kosher salt to taste

Instructions:

- Inside a large pot, cover chickpeas with several inches of cold water and set aside for 8 hours to overnight. Chickpeas should be rinsed and dried before cooking.

- Preheat the oven at 425°F.

- Combine chickpeas, olive oil, and kosher salt in a mixing bowl, spread in a single layer on a baking sheet.

- Roast for about 20 minutes, tossing every 8 minutes, till the chickpeas are golden and crisp. Toss chickpeas with a pinch of salt and set aside to cool completely.

Nutrition Per Serving: Calories 158, Fat 4.5g, Carbohydrates 23g, Protein 7.3g, Fiber 2g, Cholesterol 0mg, Sodium 42.4mg, Potassium 331mg, Phosphorus 43.5mg

21. Roasted Red Peppers

Preparation time: 5 minutes | **Cooking time:** 25 minutes | **Servings:** 4

Ingredients:

- 2 cloves of minced garlic

- 1 tablespoon of olive oil

- 3 large red bell peppers

- 1 teaspoon of Italian Seasoning

- A pinch of black pepper to taste

Instructions:

- Preheat the oven at 425° Fahrenheit.

- Wash the peppers and cut them into 1" pieces. In a mixing bowl, combine the oil, garlic, and spices.

- Roast peppers on a buttered baking sheet for around 18-20 minutes or till lightly browned and tender.

- Serve hot or cold, or use in salads or soups.

Nutrition Per Serving: Calories 73, Fat 4g, Carbohydrates 8g, Protein 1g, Fiber 1g, Cholesterol 0mg, Sodium 8mg, Potassium 272mg, Phosphorus 76mg

22. Rosemary Walnuts

Preparation time: 10 minutes | **Cooking time:** 10 minutes | **Servings:** 4

Ingredients:

- 2 cups of walnuts

- 1 tablespoon of minced fresh rosemary

- 2 cloves of minced garlic

- 1 tablespoon of honey

- 1 tablespoon of extra-virgin olive oil

Instructions:

- Preheat the oven at 350 degrees F. Line a baking sheet using parchment paper.

- Combine the walnuts, olive oil, garlic, honey, and rosemary in a mixing bowl, spread on a baking sheet lined with parchment paper.

- Inside a preheated oven, bake for about 10 minutes or till the walnuts are lightly toasted.

Nutrition Per Serving: Calories 188, Fat 18g, Carbohydrates 6g, Protein 3.9g, Fiber 3g, Cholesterol 0mg, Sodium 81mg, Potassium 116.1mg, Phosphorus 39.9mg

23. Spiced Peanut Butter Apples

Preparation time: 5 minutes | **Cooking time:** 25 minutes | **Servings:** 4

Ingredients:

- ⅛ teaspoon of ground cloves

- 4 Granny Smith apples

- ½ teaspoon of vanilla extract

- 6 tablespoons of peanut butter

- ⅛ teaspoon of ground cardamom

Instructions:

- Preheat the oven at 350 degrees F.

- Remove the apple tops using a sharp knife. Remove the cores from the apples using an apple corer, leaving the bottoms intact.

- 1 1/2 tablespoons of peanut butter and a splash of vanilla extract should be stuffed into the cored apples. In a baking dish, sprinkle cardamom and cloves over the apples.

- Bake for around 20 to 25 minutes in a preheated oven or till the apples are soft and aromatic.

Nutrition Per Serving: Calories 206, Fat 12.3g, Carbohydrates 20g, Protein 6.5g, Fiber 1g, Cholesterol 0mg, Sodium 113.6mg, Potassium 312.3mg, Phosphorus 43.5mg

24. Simple Edamame Hummus

Preparation time: 10 minutes | **Cooking time**: 0 minute | **Servings**: 6

Ingredients:

- 1/2 lemon, juiced

- 3 wedges of creamy Swiss

- Raw carrots, bell pepper, celery for dipping

- 13 oz. of steamer bag shelled edamame

- 1/2 teaspoon of each salt & pepper

Instructions:

- Heat the edamame according to the package directions. Fill the bottom of a food processor with the ingredients.

- Creamy Swiss should be cut into small pieces. To thoroughly mix the ingredients, use a pulsing motion.

- Add the juice of half a lemon and process till the mixture is creamy. Scrape the sides of the bowl with a small rubber spatula.

- Add a pinch of sea salt and black pepper to taste. Place inside a serving dish and top with vegetables.

Nutrition Per Serving: Calories 72, Total Fat 3g, Protein 5g, Carbs 6g, Fiber 3g, Cholesterol 0mg, Sodium 227mg, Potassium 137mg, Phosphorus 25mg

25. Salad Skewers

Preparation time: 10 minutes | **Cooking time**: 0 minutes | **Servings**: 4

Ingredients:

- 2 cucumbers

- 1 teaspoon of olive oil

- 2 cups of cherry tomatoes

- ½ teaspoon of lemon juice

Instructions:

- Cut the cucumbers into medium-sized pieces.

- Thread the cucumber cubes and cherry tomatoes onto the skewers one at a time.

- Finally, drizzle the salad skewers with lemon juice and olive oil.

Nutrition Per Serving: Calories 49, Fat 2g, Carbohydrates 9g, Proteins 2g, Fiber 0.1g, Cholesterol 0mg, Sodium 8mg, Potassium 435mg, Phosphorus 51mg

26. Stuffed Creamy Mushrooms

Preparation time: 10 minutes | **Cooking time:** 20 minutes | **Servings:** 6

Ingredients:

- Cooking spray

- 3 chopped garlic cloves

- 12 mushroom caps, washed and stems removed

- 4 wedges of light Swiss

- 1/2 cup of parsley, chopped

Instructions:

- Preheat the oven at 350 degrees Fahrenheit.

- Warm a large-sized skillet over medium-high flame. Spray the mushrooms using butter spray after wiping the tops clean with a damp paper towel.

- Sear the bottoms of the mushroom caps in the pan for about 2 minutes.

- Place the mushroom caps in a pie dish and set aside. Spray the pan with cooking spray and add the garlic and parsley while it's still hot.

- Remove the cheese wedges from their packaging and place them in the mixing bowl. Once the parsley and garlic are cooked, stir them into the cheese mixture in the bowl with a fork.

- After adding the mixture, bake the mushroom caps for around 12 to 15 minutes. Allow cooling slightly before serving.

Nutrition Per Serving: Calories 82, Total Fat 2g. Protein 8g. Carbs 11g, Fiber 0.5g, Cholesterol 2mg, Sodium 114mg, Potassium 69mg, Phosphorus 0mg

27. Turmeric Cauliflower Florets

Preparation time: 5 minutes | **Cooking time:** 25 minutes | **Servings:** 4

Ingredients:

- 1 tablespoon of olive oil

- 2 cups of cauliflower florets

- 1 tablespoon of ground turmeric

- 1 teaspoon of smoked paprika

Instructions:

- The cauliflower florets are seasoned with turmeric, smoked paprika, and olive oil.

- Then, using baking paper, line the baking pan in a single layer with cauliflower florets.

- Bake for around 20 minutes at 375°F, or till the cauliflower florets are soft.

Nutrition Per Serving: Calories 50, Fat 3.8g, Carbohydrates 4.1g, Protein 1.2g, Fiber 1g, Cholesterol 0mg, Sodium 16mg, Potassium 207mg, Phosphorus 43mg

28. Tossed Tomato Basil Side Salad

Preparation time: 10 minutes | **Cooking time:** 0 minute | **Servings:** 8

Ingredients:

- 2 oz. of parmesan cheese shredded

- 3 tablespoons of fresh basil, torn

- Lemon vinaigrette

- 2 cups of halved grape tomatoes

- 4 cups of green leaf lettuce

Instructions:

- Inside a medium-sized mixing bowl, combine the lettuce and basil. Finish with tomato, Parmesan, and lemon vinaigrette.

- Combine all of the ingredients and serve.

Nutrition Per Serving: Calories 107, Total Fat 9g, Protein 2g, Carbs 9g, Fiber 3g, Cholesterol 0mg, Sodium 30mg, Potassium 18mg, Phosphorus 0mg

---

29. Yummy Fresh Salsa

Preparation time: 10 minutes | **Cooking time:** 0 minute | **Servings:** 4

Ingredients:

- 1 cup of fresh cilantro

- 6 Roma tomatoes

- 1 lime juiced

- 2 pressed or minced garlic cloves

- 1 jalapeno

Instructions:

- Cut Roma tomatoes in half if using. Remove the seeds from the jalapeno and cut them in half.

- In a food processor, combine all of the ingredients. Before mixing the ingredients, pulse them in a blender or finely chop them in a food processor. Serve with fresh vegetables or on top of a lean protein source.

Nutrition Per Serving: Calories 40, Total Fat 0.1g, Protein 0.1g, Carbs 2g, Fiber 1g, Cholesterol 0mg, Sodium 256mg, Potassium 99mg, Phosphorus 18mg

---

30. Zucchini Galore

Preparation time: 5 minutes | **Cooking time:** 15 minutes | **Servings:** 3

Ingredients:

- 2 tablespoons of olive oil

- 3 zucchinis

- 1 medium-sized sweet onion

- Salt to taste

Instructions:

- Cut zucchini lengthwise into half-moons, then crosswise into thin half-moons. Using a large dicer, cut the onion into large slices. Inside a large-sized skillet over a medium-high flame, heat the oil.

- In a skillet, brown the onion in olive oil until it is lightly browned. Cook, stirring frequently, till the zucchini is softened and lightly browned. Season using salt and pepper to taste.

Nutrition Per Serving: Calories 122, Total fat 9.3g, Protein 2.7g, Carbs 9.1g, Fiber 0.1g, Cholesterol 4mg, Sodium 53mg, Potassium 91mg, Phosphorus 13mg

Chapter 7: Vegetarian Recipes

1. Arugula and Pine Nuts Salad

Preparation time: 5 minutes | **Cooking time:** 0 minutes | **Servings:** 4

Ingredients:

- 3 tablespoons of pine nuts

- 2 tablespoons of chopped chives

- 5 cups of baby arugula

- 2 tablespoons of avocado oil

- 1 tablespoon of balsamic vinegar

Instructions:

- Toss all of the ingredients inside a salad bowl and chill for 3 minutes.

Nutrition Per Serving: Calories 60, Fat 5.5g, Carbohydrates 2.2g, Protein 1.7g, Fiber 1g, Cholesterol 0mg, Sodium 7mg, Potassium 160mg, Phosphorus 43mg

2. Bake Cashew Aubergine

Preparation time: 5 minutes | **Cooking time:** 25 minutes | **Servings:** 3

Ingredients:

- 2 aubergines

- 6 tablespoons of olive oil

- 50g of finely chopped fresh coriander

- 2 minced cloves of garlic

- 100g of raw cashews

Instructions:

- Preheat the oven at 340°F.

- Cut the aubergines in half and place them cut-side up in a baking dish.

- Then drizzle with one tablespoon of olive oil and bake till the vegetables are soft. This should only take about 20 minutes.

- Inside a food processor, combine the cashews, garlic, coriander, and 5 tablespoons of olive oil till a thick paste forms.

- Thin the mixture with a little water if necessary.

- Cook for 5 minutes more under the grill with the cashew paste evenly spread over the aubergines.

- Serve with a salad of onion, tomato, and parsley or your favorite salad.

Nutrition Per Serving: Calories 344, Fat 33.5g, Carbohydrates 6g, Protein 6.3g, Fiber 0g, Cholesterol 41mg, Sodium 224mg, Potassium 721mg, Phosphorus 129mg

3. Crab Salad

Preparation time: 10 minutes | **Cooking time:** 0 minute | **Servings:** 1 small portion

Ingredients:

- 1 tablespoon of light mayonnaise

- 2 oz. of imitation crab

- 1 pinch of seafood seasoning

- 1/2 scoop of unflavored protein powder

- 1 pinch of dried dill

Instructions:

- Crab meat should be cut into very small pieces.

- Inside a mixing bowl, combine the crab meat with light mayonnaise and unflavored protein.

- Season using salt and pepper to taste.

Nutrition Per Serving: Calories 118, Total Fat 5g, Protein 13g, Carbs 8g, Fiber 0.3g, Cholesterol 98mg, Sodium 654mg, Potassium 548mg, Phosphorus 187mg

4. Carrot Cakes

Preparation time: 10 minutes | **Cooking time:** 10 minutes | **Servings:** 4

Ingredients:

- 1 beaten egg

- 1 tablespoon of sesame oil

- 1 cup of grated carrot, grated

- 1 tablespoon of semolina

- 1 teaspoon of Italian seasonings

Instructions:

- Inside a mixing bowl, combine grated carrot, semolina, egg, and Italian spices.

- Heat the sesame oil in a skillet.

- Make the carrot cakes with the help of two spoons and place them in the skillet.

- Cook the cakes for 4 minutes on each side.

Nutrition Per Serving: Calories 70, Fat 4.9g, Carbohydrates 4.8g, Protein 1.9g, Fiber 0.1g, Cholesterol 42mg, Sodium 35mg, Potassium 108mg, Phosphorus 32mg

5. Cauliflower Steaks

Preparation time: 10 minutes | **Cooking time:** 20 minutes | **Servings:** 4

Ingredients:

- 1-pound of the cauliflower head
- 1 teaspoon of ground turmeric
- ½ teaspoon of cayenne pepper
- 2 tablespoons of olive oil
- ½ teaspoon of garlic powder

Instructions:

- The cauliflower head steaks are rubbed with turmeric, cayenne pepper, and garlic powder.
- Then, line a baking sheet with baking paper and arrange the cauliflower steaks on it.
- Sprinkle with olive oil and bake for 25 minutes at 375°F, or till the veggie steaks are cooked.

Nutrition Per Serving: Calories 92, Fat 7.2g, Carbohydrates 6.8g, Protein 2.4g, Fiber 0g, Cholesterol 0mg, Sodium 34mg, Potassium 366mg, Phosphorus 91mg

6. Curry Soup

Preparation time: 5 minutes | **Cooking time:** 25 minutes | **Servings:** 4

Ingredients:

- 4 chopped celery stalks
- 8 carrots, peeled & sliced
- 1 chopped yellow onion
- 3 tablespoons of olive oil
- 2 teaspoons of curry paste

Instructions:

- Inside a saucepan, heat the oil and add the onion, celery, and carrots, stirring constantly for about 5 minutes.
- Then stir in the curry paste and water. Cook for 10 minutes more, stirring frequently.

- When all of the ingredients are soft, puree the soup till smooth, then return to the heat for another minute.

Nutrition Per Serving: Calories 171, Fat 12g, Carbohydrates 15.8g, Protein 1.6g, Fiber 0.2g, Cholesterol 0mg, Sodium 106mg, Potassium 477mg, Phosphorus 156mg

7. Cauliflower Puree

Preparation time: 5 minutes | **Cooking time:** 15 minutes | **Servings:** 4

Ingredients:

- 1 head of cauliflower, chopped into florets
- 1 tablespoon of butter
- Salt to taste

Instructions:

- In a 4-quart saucepan of salted water, cook the cauliflower for 7 to 10 minutes or till soft after draining the cauliflower, set aside 1 cup of the cooking liquid.
- In a blender, puree the cauliflower with 1/4 cup of the cooking liquid till smooth, then add more water to achieve the desired consistency. Season using salt and pepper, then pulse in the butter till thoroughly combined.

Nutrition Per Serving: Calories 61, Total Fat 3g, Protein 2.9g, Carbs 7.6g, Fiber 4g, Cholesterol 24mg, Sodium 265mg, Potassium 311mg, Phosphorus 24mg

8. Eggplant Soup

Preparation time: 5 minutes | **Cooking time:** 25 minutes | **Servings:** 4

Ingredients:

- 2 tablespoons of chopped parsley
- 1 tablespoon of olive oil
- 2 roughly cubed big eggplants
- 1 teaspoon of ground turmeric
- 2 tablespoons of tomato paste

Instructions:

- Inside a saucepan over medium flame, heat the oil, then add the eggplants and cook for 5 minutes.

- After adding the remaining ingredients and water as needed, cook the soup for another 20 minutes.

Nutrition Per Serving: Calories 108, Fat 4.1g, Carbohydrates 18.1g, Protein 3.1g, Fiber 0.1g, Cholesterol 0mg, Sodium 22mg, Potassium 735mg, Phosphorus 143mg

9. Green Bean Salad

Preparation time: 15 minutes | **Cooking time:** 5 minutes | **Servings:** 4

Ingredients:

For the Salad:

- 2 pounds of trimmed fresh green beans

- 1 bunch of chopped radishes

- 3 chopped cucumbers

For the Dressing:

- 1 tablespoon of vinegar

- 1 tablespoon of olive oil

Instructions:

- Bring a pot of water to boil, cook beans in the boiling water for 3 to 5 minutes or till bright green and slightly tender. Soak the green beans in cold water till completely cool before draining.

- Inside a large mixing bowl, combine green beans, cucumbers, and radishes.

- Inside a small-sized bowl, whisk together the olive oil and vinegar till the oil emulsifies into the vinegar, season with black pepper. Toss the salad in the dressing in a large-sized mixing bowl to coat.

Nutrition Per Serving: Calories 68, Fat 2g, Carbohydrates 12g, Proteins 3g, Fiber 0.4mg, Cholesterol 6mg, Sodium 112mg, Potassium 238mg, Phosphorus 31mg

10. Hasselback Eggplant

Preparation time: 5 minutes | **Cooking time:** 25 minutes | **Servings:** 2

Ingredients:

- 2 sliced tomatoes

- 1 tablespoon of low-fat yogurt

- 2 trimmed eggplants

- 1 teaspoon of olive oil

- 1 teaspoon of curry powder

Instructions:

- Using a knife, cut the eggplants into Hasselback shapes.

- After that, the vegetables are rubbed with curry powder and stuffed with sliced tomatoes.

- After brushing the eggplants with olive oil and yogurt, wrap them in foil (each Hasselback eggplant wraps separately).

- Preheat the oven at 375°F and bake for around 20 minutes.

Nutrition Per Serving: Calories 188, Fat 3g, Carbohydrates 18g, Protein 7g, Fiber 0g, Cholesterol 0mg, Sodium 23mg, Potassium 1580mg, Phosphorus 78mg

11. Lemony Leeks

Preparation time: 5 minutes | **Cooking time**: 25 minutes | **Servings**: 8

Ingredients:

- 1 lemon juiced

- 1/4 cup of extra-virgin olive oil

- 2 pounds of leeks, white parts only, chopped

- 1 tablespoon of sweetener

- 3 finely chopped garlic cloves

Instructions:

- Cook and stir garlic and sweetener inside a large frying pan over medium-low flame for 3 to 5 minutes or till garlic is nicely browned. Cook for about 10 minutes, stirring constantly, or till the leeks are nicely browned.

- Season using salt and pepper after drizzling lemon juice over the leek mixture. Cook for 10 to 15 minutes, covered, or till the leeks are soft.

Nutrition Per Serving: Calories 140, Total Fat 7.3g, Protein 1.8g, Carbs 14g, Fiber 2g, Cholesterol 3mg, Sodium 230mg, Potassium 63mg, Phosphorus 0mg

12. Mexican-Style Chicken Salad

Preparation time: 10 minutes | **Cooking time:** 0 minute | **Servings:** 2

Ingredients:

- 1 tablespoon of light mayonnaise

- 2 teaspoons of juice from jarred salsa without chunks

- 1 cup of drained canned chicken

- 1 teaspoon of taco seasoning

Instructions:

- Fill a dish halfway with canned chicken. Shred the chicken into small pieces with a fork. Incorporate the mayonnaise till combined and soft.

- Combine taco seasoning and salsa juice in a mixing bowl. Serve.

Nutrition Per Serving: Calories 112, Total Fat 4g, Protein 18g, Carbs 2g, Fiber 0.4g, Cholesterol 54mg, Sodium 226mg, Potassium 208mg, Phosphorus 51mg

13. Mushroom and Green Bean Casserole

Preparation time: 5 minutes | **Cooking time:** 25 minutes | **Servings:** 8

Ingredients:

- 1 package of sliced mushrooms

- 1 diced white onion

- 1 lb. of fresh green beans, trimmed & halved

- 1/2 cup of fried onions

- 1 can of fat-free cream of mushroom soup

Instructions:

- Preheat the oven at 350 degrees Fahrenheit.

- To steam the green beans, bring a saucepan of water to boil, cook for about 5 minutes, and then drain. Set aside the green beans.

- Spray a large Dutch oven with cooking spray, then add the onions. Cook till the vegetables are tender. Cook for a few minutes after adding the mushrooms.

- Stir in the fat-free cream of mushroom to combine the ingredients. Stir in the cooked green beans till they are completely covered.

- Fill an 8x8 casserole dish halfway with the ingredients. Sprinkle with fried onions on the top. Cook for about 10 minutes in the oven. Before serving, allow the food to cool completely.

Nutrition Per Serving: Calories 51, Total Fat 2g, Protein 2g, Carbs 8g, Fiber 3g, Cholesterol 1mg, Sodium 432mg, Potassium 213mg, Phosphorus 67mg

14. Roasted Parmesan Brussels Sprouts

Preparation time: 5 minutes | **Cooking time:** 20 minutes | **Servings:** 4

Ingredients:

- 2 oz. of shredded parmesan cheese

- 1/2 teaspoon of each sea salt and black pepper

- 2 teaspoons of olive oil

- 1/2 cup of low-fat grated parmesan cheese

- 1 lb. of Brussels sprouts

Instructions:

- Preheat the oven at 425°F. After removing the leaves from the Brussels sprouts, cut them in half.

- Toss with grated parmesan cheese and olive oil after seasoning with salt and pepper. Place on a baking sheet lined with foil.

- Roast Brussels sprouts for about 18 minutes in the oven. Remove from the oven and top with grated parmesan cheese. Return the dish to the oven for 2 minutes more. Remove the dish from the oven and serve.

Nutrition Per Serving: Calories 95, Total Fat 5g, Protein 6g, Carbs 5g, Fiber 4g, Cholesterol 0mg, Sodium 556mg, Potassium 483mg, Phosphorus 135mg

15. Roasted Eggplant

Preparation time: 5 minutes | **Cooking time:** 25 minutes | **Servings:** 8

Ingredients:

- 1/4 cup of olive oil

- 1/2 teaspoon of garlic powder

- Fresh parsley and basil for serving

- 2 large eggplants

- 1 teaspoon of dried basil

Instructions:

- Using a knife, cut the eggplant in half lengthwise. Each half should be cut into 6-8 wedges.

- After salting the wedges, set them aside for 30-45 minutes.

- Preheat the oven at 400 degrees Fahrenheit.

- Thoroughly rinse the eggplant and pat dry using paper towels. Place on a baking sheet and brush with olive oil.

- Season with salt, pepper, and other seasonings to taste. Cook for around 20-25 minutes or till golden brown.

Nutrition Per Serving: Calories 89, Total Fat 7g, Protein 1g, Carbs 7g, Fiber 1g, Cholesterol 0mg, Sodium 421mg, Potassium 62mg, Phosphorus 0mg

16. Sautéed Brussels Sprouts Salad

Preparation time: 5 minutes | **Cooking time:** 15 minutes | **Servings:** 4

Ingredients:

- 3 cups of shredded Brussels Sprouts

- 2 teaspoons of olive oil

- 1/4 teaspoon of each salt and pepper

Instructions:

- Set aside the quartered Brussels sprouts.

- Cooking spray a skillet and heat it on medium-high. Stir-fry the Brussels sprouts in 2 teaspoons of olive oil for a few minutes. Season with salt and pepper to taste.

- Allow the mixture to be brown and crisp, stirring occasionally. It takes approximately 8 minutes. Remove the pan from the flame and serve.

Nutrition Per Serving: Calories 113, Total Fat 7g, Protein 7g, Carbs 6g, Fiber 6g, Cholesterol 3mg, Sodium 96mg, Potassium 667mg, Phosphorus 105mg

17. Steamed Lemony Broccoli

Preparation time: 5 minutes | **Cooking time:** 10 minutes | **Servings:** 4

Ingredients:

- 2 teaspoons of lemon juice

- Salt & black pepper

- 1 pound of broccoli

- 1 tablespoon of butter

Instructions:

- Remove the broccoli florets and set aside. Large stems should be thrown away. Smaller stems should be trimmed, and larger stems should be thinly sliced. Inside a large-sized pot, bring 2 to 3 inches of water and the steamer basket to a boil. Add the broccoli and cover. Steam for 6 minutes or till crisp-tender.

- Place the broccoli inside a serving bowl. Toss in the butter and lemon juice to lightly coat. Season using salt and pepper to taste.

Nutrition Per Serving: Calories 59, Total fat 3g, Protein 3g, Carbs 6g, Fiber 2g, Cholesterol 0mg, Sodium 32mg, Potassium 229mg, Phosphorus 17mg

18. Tofu Parmigiana

Preparation time: 5 minutes | **Cooking time:** 10 minutes | **Servings:** 2

Ingredients:

- 1 teaspoon of coconut oil

- 6 oz. of roughly sliced firm tofu

- 1 teaspoon of tomato sauce

- ½ teaspoon of Italian seasonings

Instructions:

- Inside a mixing bowl, combine the tomato sauce and Italian spices.

- Then, coat the tofu slices with the tomato sauce and set aside for 10 minutes to marinate.

- Heat the coconut oil.

- Then, in the hot oil, place the sliced tofu and cook for 3 minutes on each side or till golden brown.

Nutrition Per Serving: Calories 83, Fat 6.2g, Carbohydrates 2g, Protein 7g, Fiber 0.1g, Cholesterol 1mg, Sodium 24mg, Potassium 135mg, Phosphorus 42mg

19. Zesty Squash and Zucchini

Preparation time: 5 minutes | **Cooking time:** 15 minutes | **Servings:** 4

Ingredients:

- 3 cubed small zucchinis

- 1 can of diced tomatoes with green Chile peppers

- 3 medium cubed small yellow squash

- 1/2 chopped onion

- Garlic powder to taste

Instructions:

- Combine the squash, zucchini, tomatoes, chilies, onion, and garlic powder inside a large saucepan. Bring to boil over medium-high flame.

- Reduce the flame to low and continue to cook for around 20 minutes or till the potatoes are tender and crispy.

Nutrition Per Serving: Calories 43, Fat 0.4g, Carbohydrates 9g, Protein 1.8g, Fiber 0.2g, Cholesterol 1mg, Sodium 7.5mg, Potassium 406.5mg, Phosphorus 36.1mg

20. Zucchini Soup

Preparation time: 5 minutes | **Cooking time:** 20 minutes | **Servings:** 4

Ingredients:

- 21 ounces of sliced zucchini

- 2 cloves of crushed garlic

- 1 chopped bunch of chives

- 2 chopped onions

- 3 cups of water, divided

Instructions:

- In a nonstick pan over medium flame, combine zucchini, garlic, onions, and two tablespoons of water, cook till zucchini is tender, about 5 to 10 minutes. Add the 1/2 cup of water and bring to boil. Reduce the flame to low and cook for another 5 minutes. Remove the pan from the flame and set it aside to cool.

- Fill a food processor no more than halfway with zucchini mixture, cover, and pulse a few times before blending. In batches, puree till smooth. Season with chives just before serving.

Nutrition Per Serving: Calories 57, Fat 1g, Carbohydrates 12g, Proteins 3g, Fiber 0.1g, Cholesterol 3mg, Sodium 100mg, Potassium 600mg, Phosphorus 134mg

Chapter 8: Fish and Seafood

1. Almond Pesto Salmon Fillets

Preparation time: 10 minutes | **Cooking time:** 18 minutes | **Servings:** 2

Ingredients:

- 8 oz. of salmon fillets skinless and boneless

- 1/4 cup of ground almonds

- 2 tablespoons of olive oil

- 1/4 cup of pesto marinade

- Salt & pepper to taste

Instructions:

- Combine the almonds and pesto inside a small-sized bowl. Set aside the mixture.

- Brush each fillet with oil and then top with half of the pesto mixture. Place the fillets in a hot nonstick skillet.

- Cook for approximately 12 to 15 minutes. Serve right away.

Nutrition Per Serving: Calories 433, Total Fat 34g, Protein 23.3g, Carbs 3.7g, Fiber 0g, Cholesterol 143mg, Sodium 138mg, Potassium 872mg, Phosphorus 165mg

2. BBQ Salmon

Preparation time: 5 minutes | **Cooking time:** 20 minutes | **Servings:** 4

Ingredients:

- 4 (4 oz.) of salmon fillets (thawed if using frozen)

- 2 tablespoons of grill seasoning

- 4 tablespoons of low-sugar bbq sauce

Instructions:

- If using the frozen salmon, thaw it first. If possible, let the salmon sit for 20 minutes before the cooking.

- On the stovetop, heat grill pan over high flame. Spray using nonstick cooking spray. Reduce the flame to a low setting. Brush the bbq sauce over the fish fillets.

- Cook the salmon on the grill for 5 minutes without even moving it. Cook for an additional 3-4 minutes on the other side. Serve the fish with extra barbecue sauce on the side. As you cook, sprinkle a pinch of seasoning on top.

- Brush on some more barbecue sauce and flip again. Cook for another minute. Remove them from the flame. At this point, the fish should be flaky and prepare to eat.

Nutrition Per Serving: Calories 124, Total Fat 2g, Protein 22g, Carbs 7g, Fiber 0g, Cholesterol 67mg, Sodium 310mg, Potassium 111mg, Phosphorus 31mg

3. Broiled Lobster Tail

Preparation time: 5 minutes | **Cooking time:** 15 minutes | **Servings:** 2

Ingredients:

- 1 teaspoon of parsley finely chopped

- 2 lobster tails 4-8 ounces, cold water

- 4 tablespoons of butter salted

- 2 lemon wedges

- 1 teaspoon of garlic minced

Instructions:

- Preheat the oven broiler to high and place the top rack in the oven.

- Butterfly and clean the lobster tails with kitchen shears. Remove the intestines and rinse them.

- Place the butterflied lobster tail, shell side down, on a baking dish, with the flesh closest to the top oven element. Place them aside.

- Melt two tablespoons of butter in a small microwave-safe dish for 20-30 seconds.

- Add the minced garlic and finely chopped parsley.

- Spoon the butter mixture over the lobster flesh with care. Set some aside for after you've finished cooking.

- Each lobster tail should be topped with one tablespoon of butter.

- Broil the lobster tail in the oven for 1 1/4 minutes per ounce at 4-5 inches from the flame (one minute & 15 seconds per ounce). Large tails should be broiled further away from the flame source (around 6-8 minutes)

- Remove from the oven and check for doneness (140°F) with a meat thermometer, or look for white or opaque flesh rather than transparent meat.

- Remove from the oven and top with the rest of the butter and lemon juice.

Nutrition Per Serving: Calories 285, Total Fat 23g, Protein 11g, Carbs 10g, Fiber 0g, Cholesterol 77mg, Sodium 193mg, Potassium 177mg, Phosphorus 34mg

4. Baked Crab Legs

Preparation time: 10 minutes | **Cooking time:** 20 minutes | **Servings:** 2

Ingredients:

- 4 crab Leg clusters

- 1/2 tablespoon of lemon juice

- 1/4 cup of unsalted butter

- 2 cloves of minced or pressed garlic

- 1/4 teaspoon of black pepper and sea salt each

Instructions:

- Smear two teaspoons of butter all over the crab legs inside a large-sized mixing bowl. Lay the crab legs out on a baking sheet.

- Preheat the oven at 400°F and bake for around 15 minutes.

- Melt the remaining butter inside a medium-sized saucepan and stir in the minced garlic cloves, black pepper, and salt. Remove from flame after 30 seconds of stirring till fragrant. Squeeze in the freshly squeezed lemon juice.

- Before serving, split the crab legs open and cut the meat. With a dollop of lemon butter on top, serve.

Nutrition Per Serving: Calories 553, Total Fat 40.8g, Protein 40.9g, Carbs 4.8g, Fiber 1g, Cholesterol 110mg, Sodium 760mg, Potassium 414mg, Phosphorus 98mg

5. Cajun-Flavored Salmon

Preparation time: 10 minutes | **Cooking time:** 15 minutes | **Servings:** 2

Ingredients:

- 2 teaspoons of Cajun seasoning

- 2 salmon fillet fresh and skin removed

- Salt to taste

- 2 tablespoons of olive oil

- 1/2 lemon juice for serving

Instructions:

- Season salmon fillets using salt and pepper and Cajun seasoning. Some Cajun seasoning blends contain salt, so check first before adding salt to yours.

- Warm two teaspoons of olive oil inside a nonstick skillet.

- Cook for around 8 to 10 minutes. Serve right away after squeezing the lemon over the fillets.

Nutrition Per Serving: Calories 253, Total fat 16.6g, Protein 20.9g, Carbs 1.0g, Fiber 3g, Cholesterol 47mg, Sodium 490mg, Potassium 138mg, Phosphorus 51mg

6. Foil Packed Shrimp Hobo

Preparation time: 5 minutes | **Cooking time:** 20 minutes | **Servings:** 4

Ingredients:

- 2 tablespoons of chopped cilantro

- 1 avocado

- 1 bag of frozen cauliflower rice

- 16 oz. of cleaned shrimp

- 1 lime

Instructions:

- Take four pieces of foil large enough to wrap into packages.

- Spray them lightly using nonstick frying spray.

- Put 1/4 of cauliflower rice (salt and black pepper), put 1/4 of cilantro and shrimp. Season to taste with salt and pepper.

- Cook for about 15 minutes in the oven or on the grill after folding the packets closed.

- Sprinkle with the avocado slices and lime juice.

Nutrition Per Serving: Calories 154, Total Fat 5g, Protein 31g, Carbs 7g, Fiber 1g, Cholesterol 75mg, Sodium 430mg, Potassium 233mg, Phosphorus 81mg

7. Horseradish Crusted Salmon

Preparation time: 10 minutes | **Cooking time:** 15 minutes | **Servings:** 2

Ingredients:

- 1 tablespoon of olive oil

- 8 oz. of salmon fillet

- 1 teaspoon of coconut flakes

- 2 tablespoons of horseradish, grated

- ¼ teaspoon of ground coriander

Instructions:

- Inside a mixing bowl, combine the coriander, horseradish, and coconut flakes.

- The salmon fillet should then be cut into two pieces.

- Heat the olive oil inside a skillet.

- Place the salmon fillets in a pan, then top with the horseradish mixture.

- Cook the fish for 5 minutes on medium flame.

- Cook for another 8 minutes on the other side.

Nutrition Per Serving: Calories 220, Fat 14.4g, Carbohydrates 2g, Protein 22.2g, Fiber 1g, Cholesterol 50mg, Sodium 95mg, Potassium 473mg, Phosphorus 68mg

8. Mediterranean-Style Tilapia

Preparation time: 10 minutes | **Cooking time:** 15 minutes | **Servings:** 6

Ingredients:

- 1 cup of canned Italian tomatoes diced

- 1/2 cup of crumbled feta cheese

- 1/2 cup of sliced ripe olives

- 6 tilapia fillets (6 ounces each)

- 1/2 cup of artichoke hearts water-packed chopped

Instructions:

- Preheat your oven at 390°F.

- Arrange the fillets on a baking sheet that has been greased. Arrange artichoke hearts, cheese, tomatoes, and olives on top. Preheat the oven at 350°F.

- Bake the fish for around 10 to 12 minutes or till flaky.

Nutrition Per Serving: Calories 197, Total Fat 4g, Protein 34g, Carbs 5g, Fiber 0.6g, Cholesterol 62mg, Sodium 244mg, Potassium 296mg, Phosphorus 71mg

9. Pan-Seared Scallops

Preparation time: 5 minutes | **Cooking time:** 15 minutes | **Servings:** 4

Ingredients:

- 1 tablespoon of butter

- 1 lb. of scallops

- Salt and pepper

- 1 tablespoon of olive oil

Instructions:

- Warm the cast-iron skillet over medium-high flame. Pat the scallops dry using a paper towel while you wait.

- Season the sea scallops to taste using salt and pepper.

- When the oil is hot, add the scallops, leaving enough space between them to prevent steaming.

- When you put the scallops in the pan, they should sizzle.

- Cook the scallops for about 2 minutes without moving or touching them. Using tongs, flip the scallops over and melt the butter in the pan.

- Cook the scallops for an additional minute.

- Serve the scallops right away from the pan!

Nutrition Per Serving: Calories 180, Total Fat 8g, Protein 21g, Carbs 1g, Fiber 2g, Cholesterol 45mg, Sodium 540mg, Potassium 214mg, Phosphorus 54mg

10. Peppery Flavor COD with Mixed Veggies

Preparation time: 10 minutes | **Cooking time:** 20 minutes | **Servings:** 4

Ingredients:

- 8 x 200g of cod fillets

- 100g of sun-dried tomatoes

- 500g of asparagus

- Salt & freshly ground pepper to taste

- 3 tablespoons of olive oil

Instructions:

- Preheat the oven at 400 degrees Fahrenheit.

- After 3 minutes of steaming, set the asparagus aside.

- Season both sides of the cod fillets using salt and place them on a baking tray.

- After drizzling olive oil on top, bake for about 15 minutes.

- Arrange the cod fillets with the asparagus on a bed of mixed salad and sun-dried tomatoes.

- After seasoning the fish with freshly ground pepper, serve it right away.

Nutrition Per Serving: Calories 606, Total fat 14g, Protein 78.8g, Carbs 13.2g, Fiber 0g, Cholesterol 20mg, Sodium 350mg, Potassium 197mg, Phosphorus 54mg

11. Pesto Flavored Shrimp with Summer Squash

Preparation time: 5 minutes | **Cooking time:** 20 minutes | **Servings:** 4

Ingredients:

- 1 medium sliced zucchini squash

- 1 lb. large shrimp, peeled & deveined

- 2 tablespoons of Montreal steak seasoning, divided

- 1 sliced Roma tomato and 1 medium sliced yellow squash

- 1 tablespoon of jarred pesto

Instructions:

- Add the shrimp and 1 tablespoon of seasoning together. Cook, stirring occasionally, inside a large-sized skillet over medium-high flame.

- Meanwhile, combine the squash rounds and the remaining 1 tablespoon of spice. Place the shrimp in a large mixing bowl or dish, then add the squash.

- Place the squash in the same bowl as the shrimp. Mix in the pesto sauce. Serve with sliced tomatoes on the side.

Nutrition Per Serving: Calories 112, Total Fat 3g, Protein 29g, Carbs 3g, Fiber 1g, Cholesterol 54mg, Sodium 358mg, Potassium 129mg, Phosphorus 27mg

12. Parmesan Coated Tilapia

Preparation time: 5 minutes | **Cooking time:** 20 minutes | **Servings:** 4

Ingredients:

- 4 fillets of tilapia, thawed if using frozen

- 1/2 cup of shredded non-fat parmesan cheese

- 1/4 teaspoon of dried thyme

- 1/8 teaspoon of each salt & black pepper

Instructions:

- Preheat the oven at 350°F.

- Using a paper towel, blot the fish. Grated cheese should be pressed into both sides of the fillets. Season using pepper, salt, and thyme if desired.

- Preheat a medium-sized nonstick skillet on medium flame. Cook the fish in batches in the pan for about 1 minute on each side. Fill a small-sized casserole dish halfway with the fillets.

- Bake for about 15 minutes or till the fish easily flakes.

Nutrition Per Serving: Calories 170, Total Fat 5g, Protein 24g, Carbs 3g, Fiber 0.4g, Cholesterol 34mg, Sodium 584mg, Potassium 711mg, Phosphorus 167mg

---

13. Pan-Seared Tilapia

Preparation time: 5 minutes | **Cooking time:** 15 minutes | **Servings:** 1

Ingredients:

- 1/2 tablespoon of seafood seasoning

- 2 oz. of tilapia fillet, thawed if using frozen

Instructions:

- Preheat a medium-sized nonstick skillet on medium flame.

- Season both sides of the thawed fish using seafood spice.

- Cook the fish for around 7 minutes on each side in a hot pan or till done through and flaky.

Nutrition Per Serving: Calories 61, Total Fat 1g, Protein 12g, Carbs 1g, Fiber 1g, Cholesterol 17mg, Sodium 210mg, Potassium 131mg, Phosphorus 32mg

---

14. Roasted Lemony Salmon

Preparation time: 5 minutes | **Cooking time:** 25 minutes | **Servings:** 4

Ingredients:

- 1 lemon

- 16 oz. of salmon

- Salt and pepper to taste

Instructions:

- Divide the fish into four equal pieces.

- Preheat the oven at 450 degrees Fahrenheit.

- Season the salmon to taste using salt and black pepper. Place the salmon on a nonstick baking sheet or skillet, skin side down.

- Serve the salmon with a small slice of lemon on the side.

- Cook for around 13–20 minutes or till the fish is done.

Nutrition Per Serving: Calories 100, Total Fat 2g, Protein 20g, Carbs 1g, Fiber 0.3g, Cholesterol 52mg, Sodium 360mg, Potassium 442mg, Phosphorus 117mg

---

15. Shrimp Cocktail Dip

Preparation time: 5 minutes | **Cooking time:** 20 minutes | **Servings:** 24 (3 cups)

Ingredients:

- 2 green onions sliced

- 1 package of cream cheese softened (8 ounces)

- 3/4 cup of cocktail sauce

- 1/4 cup of Parmesan cheese grated

- 3/4 pound of shrimp, chopped, cleaned, and cooked

Instructions:

- Cream cheese should be spread on the bottom of a small oven-safe glass bowl.

- Combine the cocktail sauce and shrimp in a mixing cup and spread over the cream cheese mixture. Garnish with parmesan and green onions.

- Bake for about 15 minutes at 350°F or till the cheese melts.

Nutrition Per Serving: Calories 54, Total Fat 3.2g, Protein 4.1g, Carbs 2.2g, Fiber 0.3g, Cholesterol 11mg, Sodium 195mg, Potassium 55mg, Phosphorus 14mg

---

16. Sesame-Crusted Tuna Steaks

Preparation time: 5 minutes | **Cooking time:** 15 minutes | **Servings:** 2

Ingredients:

- 2 Ahi tuna steaks

- 2 teaspoons of black sesame seeds and white sesame seeds each

- Salt and pepper to taste

- 1/2 teaspoon of garlic powder

- 1 tablespoon of sesame oil

Instructions:

- Drizzle a thin layer of oil and garlic powder over each tuna steak.

- Inside a large-sized mixing bowl, combine the pepper, salt, and sesame seeds, then press each tuna steak as deeply as possible into the mixture. Place the tuna on a nonstick pan that has been preheated.

- Cook for around 8 to 10 minutes over medium flame. Flip the steaks halfway through the cooking time.

Nutrition Per Serving: Calories 280, Total Fat 10g, Protein 42.7g, Carbs 1.2g, Fiber 7g, Cholesterol 85mg, Sodium 640mg, Potassium 210mg, Phosphorus 54mg

17. Simple Shrimp

Preparation time: 5 minutes | **Cooking time:** 10 minutes | **Servings:** 4

Ingredients:

- 1 lb. of dry & clean shrimp

- Olive oil

- Salt and black pepper

Instructions:

- Season your shrimp using salt and black pepper after thoroughly drying them.

- Heat the olive oil inside a pan over high flame.

- Cook the shrimp. On both sides, the shrimp should be pink and firm.

Nutrition Per Serving: Calories 67, Total Fat 2g, Protein 28g, Carbs 0g, Fiber 0g, Cholesterol 38mg, Sodium 560mg, Potassium 145mg, Phosphorus 43mg

18. Salmon with Basil Sauce

Preparation time: 10 minutes | **Cooking time:** 15 minutes | **Servings:** 4

Ingredients:

- 4 salmon steaks (approx. 200g each)

- 200g of fresh basil

- Salt & ground black pepper to taste

- 2 lemons juice
- 5 tablespoons of olive oil

Instructions:

- Remove the basil leaves from their stalks and pulse till smooth inside a food processor.
- To taste, add the lemon juice, salt, and black pepper. Drizzle in the olive oil slowly and set aside.
- Brush the steaks using olive oil and grill for around 10 minutes.
- Serve with a side of basil sauce.

Nutrition Per Serving: Calories 274, Total fat 24.1g, Protein 13.9g, Carbs 4.4g, Fiber 0g, Cholesterol 45mg, Sodium 400mg, Potassium 167mg, Phosphorus 36mg

19. Salmon with Cranberry Chutney Glazed

Preparation time: 10 minutes | **Cooking time:** 10 minutes | **Servings:** 4

Ingredients:

- 1/4 cup of cranberry chutney
- 1/2 teaspoon of salt (optional)
- 4 salmon fillets skinless (around 5 to 6 ounces each)
- 1/2 teaspoon of ground cinnamon
- 1 tablespoon of white wine vinegar
- 1/4 teaspoon of ground red pepper

Instructions:

- Prepare the grill for indirect grilling or preheat the broiler. Combine cinnamon, salt, and ground red pepper inside a small-sized bowl, sprinkle over fish. Combine the chutney and vinegar inside a small-sized mixing bowl, brush a small amount evenly across each salmon fillet. 2.
- Broil 5 to 6 inches away from the heat source, or grill for 4 to 6 minutes on medium-hot coals on a covered grill till the salmon is opaque in the center.

Nutrition Per Serving: Calories 229, Total fat 9g, Protein 28g, Carbs 7g, Fiber 2g, Cholesterol 61mg, Sodium 451mg, Potassium 257mg, Phosphorus 91mg

20. Tasty Chili Prawns

Preparation time: 10 minutes | **Cooking time:** 10 minutes | **Servings:** 4

Ingredients:

- 2 tablespoons of sweet chili sauce

- 3 tablespoons of olive oil

- 1 lemon juice

- 300g of tiger or king prawns cooked

- 1 tablespoon of Dijon mustard

Instructions:

- To make the prawn marinade, combine the olive oil, lemon juice, Dijon mustard, and sweet chili sauce inside a mixing bowl.

- Once the marinade has reached a uniform texture and color, add the prawns.

- Toss the prawns in the sauce till fully coated.

- Refrigerate for an hour. Overnight is the most convenient option.

- String the marinated prawns onto skewers.

- Grill the skewered prawns for 5 minutes or till the outsides begin to caramelize.

Nutrition Per Serving: Calories 162, Total fat 11.3g, Protein 13.5g, Carbs 2.2g, Fiber 0.2g, Cholesterol 64mg, Sodium 266mg, Potassium 361mg, Phosphorus 123mg

Chapter 9: Poultry Recipes

1. Apple Chicken

Preparation time: 5 minutes | **Cooking time:** 25 minutes | **Servings:** 4

Ingredients:

- 1 cup of chopped apples

- ½ cup of apple juice

- 4 chicken thighs, skinless and boneless

- 1 teaspoon of margarine

- ½ teaspoon of ground black pepper

Instructions:

- Melt the margarine inside a saucepan.

- Cook the chicken for 5 minutes on each side.

- Then add the remaining ingredients with 1/2 cup of water and close the lid.

- Cook the chicken for 20 minutes on low flame.

Nutrition Per Serving: Calories 330, Fat 12g, Carbohydrates 11g, Protein 43g, Fiber 0.2g, Cholesterol 130mg, Sodium 139mg, Potassium 449mg, Phosphorus 145mg

2. Asparagus and Mozzarella Stuffed Chicken

Preparation time: 5 minutes | **Cooking time:** 15 minutes | **Servings:** 4

Ingredients:

- 8 asparagus spears trimmed, divided

- 1/2 cup of grated skim-part mozzarella cheese, divided

- 2 large halves of chicken breast boneless and skinless

- 1/4 cup of Italian seasoned whole-wheat bread crumbs

- A pinch of black pepper to taste

Instructions:

- Preheat oven at 400 degrees Fahrenheit.

- Place each chicken breast between two heavy plastic sheets on a sturdy, flat surface. Pound the chicken to an equal thickness of 1/4 inch with the smooth side of a meat mallet. On both sides, season using pepper and salt.

- In the center of a chicken breast, place four asparagus stalks and 1/4 cup of mozzarella cheese. Roll the leftover chicken breasts around the asparagus and cheese to make a neat, compact roll. Sprinkle the crumbs over the prepared baking sheet.

- Bake for approximately 20 minutes.

Nutrition Per Serving: Calories 390, Fat 10.8g, Carbohydrates 11g, Protein 57.4g, Fiber 0.5g, Cholesterol 147mg, Sodium 181mg, Potassium 542mg, Phosphorus 59.5mg

3. Baked Glazed Chicken

Preparation time: 5 minutes | **Cooking time:** 25 minutes | **Servings:** 4

Ingredients:

- 3 tablespoons of low-sodium hot chili sauce

- 4 chicken thighs, boneless & skinless

- ½ cup of balsamic vinegar

- 3 tablespoons of garlic, minced

- 1 teaspoon of ground black pepper

Instructions:

- Pour the oil into a baking dish, then add the chicken and the remaining ingredients.

- Toss well and bake for about 25 minutes at 450°F.

Nutrition Per Serving: Calories 286, Fat 11g, Carbohydrates 1.4g, Protein 42.5g, Fiber 0g, Cholesterol 130mg, Sodium 270mg, Potassium 389mg, Phosphorus 142mg

4. Baked Chicken with Salsa and Guacamole

Preparation time: 5 minutes | **Cooking time:** 20 minutes | **Servings:** 3

Ingredients:

- 3 breasts of chicken boneless

- 1/2 cup of grated skim-part Cheddar cheese

- 3 tablespoons of guacamole

- 1/3 cup of salsa

- A pinch of ground black pepper to taste

Instructions:

- Preheat the oven at 380 degrees Fahrenheit. Grease a baking pan using cooking spray.

- In a baking pan, season the chicken with pepper. Spread salsa on the chicken breasts and then top with cheddar cheese.

- Bake the chicken for about 15 minutes or till golden brown.

- Spread 1 tablespoon of guacamole on each chicken breast before serving.

Nutrition Per Serving: Calories 298, Fat 18g, Carbohydrates 10g, Protein 24.2g, Fiber 0g, Cholesterol 84.4mg, Sodium 151mg, Potassium 325.2mg, Phosphorus 32.2mg

5. Baked Chicken with Mixed Veggies

Preparation time: 10 minutes | **Cooking time:** 20 minutes | **Servings:** 4

Ingredients:

- 1 cup of mixed vegetables

- 4 chicken breasts

- 1 cup of diced sweet potatoes

- 2 tablespoons of olive oil

- Sprigs of rosemary

Instructions:

- Preheat your oven at 380 degrees Fahrenheit.

- Line a baking sheet using parchment paper.

- Drizzle an olive oil tablespoon over the chicken breasts in a baking dish.

- In a preheated oven, bake the chicken breasts for around 15 to 20 minutes or till golden brown.

- Meanwhile, heat half a kettle of water to boil, then add the dried sweet potato and cook for 5 minutes.

- Before pan-frying the sweet potato with rosemary sprigs, season it using black pepper.

- Serve the chicken with pan-fried sweet potato and your choice of boiling mixed vegetables!

Nutrition Per Serving: Calories 455, Fat 9.4g, Carbohydrates 22.2g, Protein 47g, Fiber 0g, Cholesterol 69.2mg, Sodium 123mg, Potassium 1153mg, Phosphorus 71.1mg

6. BBQ Chicken and Veggies Foil Packets

Preparation time: 5 minutes | **Cooking time**: 25 minutes | **Servings**: 4

Ingredients:

- 1 green bell pepper strips

- 1/4 teaspoon of each salt and pepper

- 1 lb. of boneless and skinless chicken breasts, cut into 1/2-inch-thick slices

- 4 tablespoons of low sugar barbecue sauce

- 1 red bell pepper, cut into strips

Instructions:

- Preheat the grill to medium flame. Close the lid till you're ready to use it.

- Cooking Spray four large pieces of foil, layer chicken, salt and black pepper, vegetables, and barbecue sauce on the foil. To close the packs, fold the foil in half.

- Cook for around 18-20 minutes or till the chicken is thoroughly cooked (165F). Before carefully opening the packets, poke holes in the foil to allow steam to escape.

- Remove with tongs from the pan and set aside to cool before serving.

Nutrition Per Serving: Calories 151, Total Fat 1g, Protein 26g, Carbs 8g, Fiber 0.1g, Cholesterol 76mg, Sodium 212mg, Potassium 193mg, Phosphorus 17mg

7. Chicken with Asparagus

Preparation time: 5 minutes | **Cooking time**: 25 minutes | **Servings**: 4

Ingredients:

- 1-pound of chicken breast, skinless and boneless, chopped

- 1 cup trimmed and halved asparagus

- 2 tablespoons of avocado oil

- ½ teaspoon of smoked paprika

- 2 cups of chopped tomatoes

Instructions:

- Heat the oil inside a skillet over medium-high flame, then add the chicken and asparagus, swirl, and cook for about 5 minutes.

- Cook with the remaining ingredients and 1 cup of water for about 20 minutes on medium-high flame.

Nutrition Per Serving: Calories 162, Fat 4g, Carbohydrates 5g, Protein 26g, Fiber 0.2g, Cholesterol 73mg, Sodium 63mg, Potassium 729mg, Phosphorus 176mg

8. Chicken Breast Stuffed with Basil

Preparation time: 5 minutes | **Cooking time:** 25 minutes | **Servings:** 4

Ingredients:

- 1 teaspoon of minced garlic

- 1-pound of chicken breast, skinless and boneless

- 2 tablespoons of basil leaves

- 1 sliced tomato

- 1 tablespoon of sesame oil

Instructions:

- Make a lengthwise cut in the chicken breast.

- Following that, the chicken breasts are rubbed with minced garlic and powdered black pepper before being stuffed with basil leaves and tomato slices.

- Toothpicks are used to keep the cut closed.

- After that, brush the chicken breast with sesame oil and wrap it in foil.

- Preheat the oven at 450 degrees Fahrenheit and bake the chicken for about 20 minutes.

Nutrition Per Serving: Calories 166, Fat 6.3g, Carbohydrates 2g, Protein 24.5g, Fiber 2.4g, Cholesterol 73mg, Sodium 59mg, Potassium 487mg, Phosphorus 172mg

9. Chicken Tomato Stew

Preparation time: 5 minutes | **Cooking time:** 25 minutes | **Servings:** 4

Ingredients:

- 10 oz. of chicken fillet, chopped
- 1 cup of chopped tomatoes
- 1 chopped chili pepper
- 2 chopped sweet peppers
- 1 teaspoon of olive oil

Instructions:

- Heat the olive oil inside a skillet.
- Now add the sweet and chili peppers. Roast the vegetables for about 3 minutes.
- Then add the chicken and cook for another 10 minutes.
- Mix in the tomatoes and 1 cup of water.
- Cook for another 10 minutes after thoroughly stirring the stew.

Nutrition Per Serving: Calories 172, Fat 7g, Carbohydrates 6g, Protein 21.5g, Fiber 0g, Cholesterol 63mg, Sodium 65mg, Potassium 393mg, Phosphorus 76mg

10. Curried Chicken Wings

Preparation time: 5 minutes | **Cooking time:** 25 minutes | **Servings:** 4

Ingredients:

- 1 tablespoon of coconut oil
- ½ cup skim milk
- 1-pound of chicken wings, skinless and boneless
- 1 teaspoon of curry paste

Instructions:

- In a blender, combine the skim milk and curry paste till smooth.

- The coconut oil is then heated in the same saucepan.

- After adding the chicken wings to the pan, cook them for about 2 minutes on each side.

- Then, whisk in the curry paste mixture with the chicken.

- Cook for about 20 minutes on medium flame with the lid closed.

Nutrition Per Serving: Calories 264, Fat 12.5g, Carbohydrates 2g, Protein 34g, Fiber 1g, Cholesterol 102mg, Sodium 114mg, Potassium 323mg, Phosphorus 124mg

11. Chicken with Lemon Glazed

Preparation time: 10 minutes | **Cooking time:** 20 minutes | **Servings:** 4

Ingredients:

- 2 teaspoons of garlic, peeled & finely chopped

- 1 green bell pepper, sliced into squares

- 4 skinless chicken breasts

- 1 tablespoon of Dijon mustard

- 2 lemons juice and zest

Instructions:

- Preheat the oven at 400 degrees Fahrenheit.

- Chicken breasts should be cut into bite-size pieces.

- Before adding the chicken, warm a spoonful of oil in a frying pan. Cook the chicken for about 5 minutes or till it is completely white.

- Inside a mixing bowl, combine the garlic, mustard, and lemon zest, and marinate the chicken for about an hour.

- In a preheated oven, bake the marinated chicken for about 20 minutes in an ovenproof dish.

- Serve with your favorite summer vegetables on the side.

Nutrition Per Serving: Calories 208, Fat 10g, Carbohydrates 4g, Protein 30.3g, Fiber 0g, Cholesterol 126mg, Sodium 102mg, Potassium 284mg, Phosphorus 62mg

12. Chicken with Carrot

Preparation time: 5 minutes | **Cooking time:** 25 minutes | **Servings:** 4

Ingredients:

- 1 cup of shredded carrot

- 4 chicken thighs, skinless and boneless

- 1 chopped onion

- 1 tablespoon of margarine and minced garlic each

- ½ teaspoon of chili flakes

Instructions:

- Melt the margarine inside a saucepan and add the onion. Cook for about 5 minutes.

- Then whisk in the remaining ingredients thoroughly and 1 cup of water.

- Cook for approximately 25 minutes on low flame with the lid closed.

Nutrition Per Serving: Calories 307, Fat 12.3g, Carbohydrates 4g, Protein 43g, Fiber 0.1g, Cholesterol 130mg, Sodium 154mg, Potassium 442mg, Phosphorus 175mg

13. Chicken with Pumpkin

Preparation time: 5 minutes | **Cooking time:** 25 minutes | **Servings:** 4

Ingredients:

- 1 tablespoon of sesame oil

- 2 cups of water

- 1 pound of chicken breasts, skinless and boneless, chopped

- 1 cup of chopped butternut squash

- 1 teaspoon of cayenne pepper

Instructions:

- Heat the oil inside a pan over medium-high flame, then add the chicken and cook for around 5 minutes.

- After adding the remaining ingredients and 1 cup of water, cook the food for about 20 minutes.

Nutrition Per Serving: Calories 263, Fat 12g, Carbohydrates 4.3g, Protein 33.2g, Fiber 0.1g, Cholesterol 101mg, Sodium 103mg, Potassium 409mg, Phosphorus 117mg

---

14. Chicken and Asparagus

Preparation time: 5 minutes | **Cooking time:** 25 minutes | **Servings:** 4

Ingredients:

- 2 cups of chopped tomatoes

- ½ teaspoon of smoked paprika

- 1 cup trimmed and halved asparagus

- 2 tablespoons of avocado oil

- 1-pound of chicken breast, skinless and boneless, chopped

Instructions:

- Heat the oil inside a skillet over medium-high flame, then add the chicken and asparagus, swirl, and cook for about 5 minutes.

- Cook the remaining ingredients after adding 1 1/2 cups of water for about 20 minutes on medium-high flame.

Nutrition Per Serving: Calories 162, Fat 4g, Carbohydrates 5g, Protein 26g, Fiber 0.2g, Cholesterol 73mg, Sodium 63mg, Potassium 729mg, Phosphorus 213mg

---

15. Creamy Turkey

Preparation time: 5 minutes | **Cooking time:** 25 minutes | **Servings:** 4

Ingredients:

- 1 cup of almond milk

- 12 oz. of turkey fillet, chopped

- 1 tablespoon of olive oil

- 2 cups of chopped broccoli

- 1 teaspoon of curry powder

Instructions:

- Heat the oil in a pan over medium-high flame, then add the turkey, curry powder, and broccoli. Stir the ingredients together for 10 minutes.

- Cook for another 15 minutes after adding the almond milk and 1/2 cup of water.

Nutrition Per Serving: Calories 160, Fat 5.2g, Carbohydrates 7g, Protein 21g, Fiber 0g, Cholesterol 44mg, Sodium 139mg, Potassium 224mg, Phosphorus 143mg

16. Five-Spices Chicken Wings

Preparation time: 5 minutes | **Cooking time:** 25 minutes | **Servings:** 4

Ingredients:

- 1 tablespoon of five-spices

- 1-pound of chicken wings, skinless and boneless

- 2 tablespoons of melted margarine

- Pinch of salt and pepper

Instructions:

- Season the chicken wings with five spices, salt, pepper, and a smear of margarine.

- Preheat the oven at 365 degrees Fahrenheit and bake the chicken wings for about 25 minutes.

Nutrition Per Serving: Calories 272, Fat 14.1g, Carbohydrates 2g, Protein 33g, Fiber 0g, Cholesterol 101mg, Sodium 195mg, Potassium 279mg, Phosphorus 63mg

17. Fajita Flavor Grilled Chicken

Preparation time: 5 minutes | **Cooking time:** 10 minutes | **Servings:** 2

Ingredients:

- 2 teaspoons of fajita seasoning mix

- 1 bunch of green onions, ends trimmed

- 2 boneless and skinless chicken breasts (around 4 ounces each)

- 1 tablespoon of olive oil

Instructions:

- Prepare your grill for direct cooking.

- Drizzle the chicken and green onions with oil. Season both sides of the chicken breasts with a spice mixture. Grill for around 6 to 8 minutes or till the chicken is no longer pink in the center.

- To serve, toss the chicken with the onions.

Nutrition Per Serving: Calories 176, Total fat 8g, Protein 19g, Carbs 8g, Fiber 0.1g, Cholesterol 24mg, Sodium 413mg, Potassium 611mg, Phosphorus 182mg

18. Grilled South of the Border Chicken

Preparation time: 5 minutes | **Cooking time:** 20 minutes | **Servings:** 4

Ingredients:

- 2 teaspoons of lemon juice

- 1/2 cup of low-fat sour cream

- 4 small skinless and boneless chicken breasts

- 1 packet of taco seasoning (search for reduced-sodium taco seasoning.)

Instructions:

- Inside a medium-sized mixing bowl, combine lemon juice, sour cream, and taco seasoning using a wire whisk. Rinse and pat dry the chicken breasts before cooking. Coat the chicken breasts evenly in the sour cream mixture. Grill the breasts for 10 minutes per side or till done. Prepare the food.

If you don't have a grill, you can cook the chicken breasts on the stovetop in a skillet sprayed using nonstick cooking spray over medium to medium-low flame.

Nutrition Per Serving: Calories 201, Total fat 7g, Protein 26g, Carbs 5g, Fiber 0g, Cholesterol 66mg, Sodium 226mg, Potassium 330mg, Phosphorus 102mg

---

19. Grilled Balsamic Chicken

Preparation time: 5 minutes | **Cooking time:** 20 minutes | **Servings:** 4

Ingredients:

- 1/2 cup of balsamic vinegar

- 1 lb. of boneless and skinless chicken breasts

- Pinch of salt

- 1 teaspoon of poultry seasoning

Instructions:

- Preheat the outdoor grill at 350°F.

- Remove any unwanted parts from the chicken breasts and season using poultry seasoning and salt on all sides. While the grill heats up, set it aside.

- Grill the chicken breast for about 5-6 minutes on each side. Check that the temperature has reached 160 degrees Fahrenheit before turning off the grill.

- While the chicken is cooking or resting, heat the vinegar inside a small-sized saucepan over medium-low flame. Bring to a gentle simmer, whisking constantly, till the sauce thickens. The glaze may take up to 10 minutes to reduce by half.

- Remove the vinegar from the flame and drizzle it over the grilled chicken. It can also be stored in a heat-resistant container.

Nutrition Per Serving: Calories 159, Total Fat 3g, Protein 24g, Carbs 6g, Fiber 0.2g, Cholesterol 74mg, Sodium 184mg, Potassium 260mg, Phosphorus 115mg

---

20. Honey Butter Chicken

Preparation time: 10 minutes | **Cooking time:** 15 minutes | **Servings:** 4

Ingredients:

- 2 tablespoons of butter

- 4 breast fillet of chicken

- 2 tablespoons of honey

- 1 teaspoon of garlic minced

- 1/2 teaspoon of ground coriander

Instructions:

- Combine the honey, melted butter, coriander, and garlic inside a large non-reactive mixing bowl. Toss everything together thoroughly after adding the chicken fillets. Allow at least one hour for marinating.

- Grill the chicken fillets for about 15 minutes or till done to your liking.

Nutrition Per Serving: Calories 235, Fat 8.8g, Carbohydrates 9g, Protein 29.1g, Fiber 0.3g, Cholesterol 130mg, Sodium 77mg, Potassium 294mg, Phosphorus 98mg

21. Marinated Teriyaki Chicken

Preparation time: 5 minutes | **Cooking time**: 20 minutes | **Servings**: 4

Ingredients:

- 1/4 cup of teriyaki marinade

- 1/4 teaspoon of black pepper

- 4 (4 oz.) of boneless and skinless chicken breast cut in 1/2 or pound out meat if thicker than 1-inch

- 1/4 teaspoon of sea salt

Instructions:

- Arrange chicken breasts in a single layer in a shallow dish. Season the chicken with salt and black pepper before drizzling the marinade over it. Turn the chicken in the dish with a fork to coat it evenly. Cover and chill for 20-30 minutes.

- Heat a nonstick grill pan over medium-high flame. Drizzle with 1 tablespoon of olive oil.

- Take the chicken out of the marinade. In a hot pan, cook the chicken breast for 5 minutes. Cook for another 5 minutes on the other side. Using a meat thermometer, check that the internal temperature of the meat is 165°F.

- Place the chicken on a cutting board and slice it thinly. Before serving, drizzle with marinade.

Nutrition Per Serving: Calories 126, Total Fat 3g, Protein 24g, Carbs 3g, Fiber 0g, Cholesterol 70mg, Sodium 440mg, Potassium 259mg, Phosphorus 194mg

22. Oregano-Flavor Turkey Tenders

Preparation time: 10 minutes | **Cooking time:** 10 minutes | **Servings:** 4

Ingredients:

- 1 tablespoon of dried oregano

- 2 turkey breast fillets, skinless and boneless

- 1 tablespoon of olive oil

- Pinch of salt

Instructions:

- Season the turkey tenderloins with olive oil and dried oregano after cutting them into tenders.

- Place the turkey tenders in a single layer in the skillet and cook for 5 minutes on each side or till golden brown.

Nutrition Per Serving: Calories 101, Fat 4.8g, Carbohydrates 1g, Protein 13.5g, Fiber 0g, Cholesterol 30mg, Sodium 40mg, Potassium 240mg, Phosphorus 47mg

23. Onion Chicken

Preparation time: 5 minutes | **Cooking time:** 25 minutes | **Servings:** 4

Ingredients:

- 1 tablespoon of chopped parsley

- 1-pound of chicken breast, skinless and boneless

- ½ teaspoon of dried oregano

- 1 cup of chopped onion

- 3 tablespoons of olive oil

Instructions:

- Add 2 tablespoons of oil inside a pan on medium-low flame, then add the onion and cook for 5 minutes.

- Continue to simmer the dish for another 10 minutes after adding the remaining ingredients, except the water.

- Then add the 1 cup of water and cook for about 15 minutes, stirring constantly.

Nutrition Per Serving: Calories 232, Fat 13.4g, Carbohydrates 3g, Protein 24.4g, Fiber 1g, Cholesterol 73mg, Sodium 61mg, Potassium 471mg, Phosphorus 123mg

24. Pesto Chicken Skewers

Preparation time: 5 minutes | **Cooking time:** 15 minutes | **Servings:** 4

Ingredients:

- 3 tablespoons of jarred pesto

- 1 lb. of boneless and skinless chicken tenderloin, cut into 1 1/2 inch pieces

- 2 cups of cherry tomatoes

- 12 leaves of fresh basil, optional

Instructions:

- Preheat the grill at medium-high temperature. Toss the chicken and tomatoes with the pesto to coat evenly.

- Thread chicken and tomatoes onto skewers in alternate directions, finishing with 3-4 basil leaves per skewer. (If using wooden skewers, soak them for 30 minutes before using.)

- Grill for 5 minutes per side or till the chicken is cooked through.

Nutrition Per Serving: Calories 350, Total Fat 8g, Protein 25g, Carbs 11g, Fiber 0g, Cholesterol 60mg, Sodium 690mg, Potassium 243mg, Phosphorus 68mg

25. Turkey with Bok Choy

Preparation time: 5 minutes | **Cooking time:** 25 minutes | **Servings:** 4

Ingredients:

- 2 tablespoons of olive oil

- 8 oz. of sliced turkey fillet

- 1 pound of chopped bok choy

- 2 tablespoons of chopped chives

- 1 teaspoon of minced ginger

Instructions:

- Heat the olive oil inside a skillet.

- Roast the ingredients for about 5 minutes after adding the turkey and ginger.

- Then add the 1 1/2 cups of water and chives, cover, and cook for about 15 minutes.

- Cook for another 5 minutes after stirring in the bok choy.

Nutrition Per Serving: Calories 130, Fat 7.5g, Carbohydrates 3g, Protein 13.6g, Fiber 0g, Cholesterol 29mg, Sodium 203mg, Potassium 297mg, Phosphorus 46mg

26. Turkey with Olives

Preparation time: 5 minutes | **Cooking time:** 25 minutes | **Servings:** 4

Ingredients:

- 1 cup of tomato puree

- 1 pound of turkey fillet, sliced

- 1 cup of green olives, pitted & halved

- 1 tablespoon of olive oil

- 1 tablespoon of chopped parsley

Instructions:

- Grease a baking dish using the oil.

- Combine the remaining ingredients inside a baking pan, flatten well, and cover using foil.

- Preheat the oven at 450°F and bake for about 25 minutes.

Nutrition Per Serving: Calories 200, Fat 8g, Carbohydrates 8g, Protein 25g, Fiber 0.6g, Cholesterol 59mg, Sodium 168mg, Potassium 282mg, Phosphorus 68mg

27. Turkey Parsnip

Preparation time: 5 minutes | **Cooking time:** 25 minutes | **Servings:** 4

Ingredients:

- 2 chopped parsnips

- 12 oz. of turkey fillet, sliced

- 1 chopped onion

- 2 tablespoons of sesame oil

- 1 tablespoon of chopped parsley

Instructions:

- Inside a pan over medium flame, heat the oil, then add the onion and cook for 5 minutes.

- Cook for another 5 minutes after adding the turkey.

- Cook for about 15 minutes after adding the remaining ingredients and 1 cup of water to the pot.

Nutrition Per Serving: Calories 177, Fat 7.3g, Carbohydrates 8.6g, Protein 18.4g, Fiber 0.1g, Cholesterol 44mg, Sodium 99mg, Potassium 171mg, Phosphorus 65mg

28. Thai-Styled Chicken Chunks

Preparation time: 5 minutes | **Cooking time:** 25 minutes | **Servings:** 4

Ingredients:

- 1 tablespoon of chopped scallions

- 16 oz. of chicken fillet, cubed

- ½ cup of low-sodium Thai chili sauce

Instructions:

- Heat a pan over medium-high flame, then add the chicken and cook for 5 minutes on each side. Place the chicken in a baking dish, stir in the chili sauce and scallions, and bake at 390°F.

- Bake for approximately 20 minutes.

Nutrition Per Serving: Calories 145, Fat 6g, Carbohydrates 1g, Protein 22g, Fiber 0.4g, Cholesterol 67mg, Sodium 70mg, Potassium 186mg, Phosphorus 67mg

29. Turkey with Savoy Cabbage

Preparation time: 5 minutes | **Cooking time:** 25 minutes | **Servings:** 4

Ingredients:

- 1 tablespoon of margarine

- 10 oz. of turkey fillet, sliced

- 1 cup of shredded Savoy cabbage

- 1 tablespoon of olive oil

- 1 teaspoon of chili powder

Instructions:

- Wrap the baking pan in foil and add all of the ingredients.

- Preheat the oven to 385°F and bake for about 25 minutes.

Nutrition Per Serving: Calories 129, Fat 7g, Carbohydrates 2g, Protein 15g, Fiber 1g, Cholesterol 37mg, Sodium 105mg, Potassium 244mg, Phosphorus 98mg

30. Turkey Gravy with Peaches

Preparation time: 5 minutes | **Cooking time:** 25 minutes | **Servings:** 4

Ingredients:

- 1 cup of peaches, chopped

- 1 tablespoon of olive oil

- 1-pound of turkey fillet, chopped

- 1 teaspoon of chili powder

- 1 teaspoon of ground paprika

Instructions:

- Roast the turkey in a pot with olive oil for about 5 minutes.

- Then thoroughly whisk in the remaining ingredients.

- Cook the dish for about 20 minutes on medium flame.

Nutrition Per Serving: Calories 155, Fat 4.3g, Carbohydrates 4.2g, Protein 24.1g, Fiber 0.4g, Cholesterol 59mg, Sodium 96mg, Potassium 264mg, Phosphorus 111mg

Chapter 10: Beef and Pork Recipes

1. Beef Loin with Sage

Preparation time: 10 minutes | **Cooking time:** 20 minutes | **Servings:** 2

Ingredients:

- 10 oz. of beef loin, strips

- 1 garlic clove, diced

- 2 tablespoons of margarine

- Pinch of salt

- 1 teaspoon of dried sage

Instructions:

- Melt the margarine in a skillet.

- Roast the garlic and dried sage for 2 minutes on low flame.

- Season the beef loin strips with salt and roast for about 15 minutes on medium flame. Stir the meat every now and then.

Nutrition Per Serving: Calories 363, Fat 23.2g, Carbohydrates 1g, Protein 38g, Fiber 1.4g, Cholesterol 101mg, Sodium 211mg, Potassium 497mg, Phosphorus 184mg

2. Beef Bites Melted

Preparation time: 5 minutes | **Cooking time:** 25 minutes | **Servings:** 4

Ingredients:

- 1 tablespoon of tomato paste

- 1 teaspoon of peppercorns

- 1-pound beef of chopped tenderloin, chopped

- 1 teaspoon of dried rosemary

- 1 teaspoon of margarine

Instructions:

- Inside a small-sized saucepan, melt the margarine.

- Roast it for about 5 minutes after adding the chopped beef.

- After that, add the peppercorns, rosemary, and tomato paste. Everything should be thoroughly combined.

- Close the lid and fill it with 1 cup of water.

- Cook the beef for approximately 20 minutes on medium-high flame.

Nutrition Per Serving: Calories 180, Fat 6.5g, Carbohydrates 1g, Protein 27.7g, Fiber 0.7mg, Cholesterol 81mg, Sodium 75mg, Potassium 407mg, Phosphorus 142mg

3. Beef Skillet

Preparation time: 5 minutes | **Cooking time:** 25 minutes | **Servings:** 3

Ingredients:

- 1 cup of sliced bell pepper

- 2 chopped tomatoes

- 1 cup of lean ground beef

- 1 chopped chili pepper

- 1 tablespoon of olive oil

Instructions:

- Heat the olive oil in a skillet and add the lean ground beef.

- It needs to be roasted for 10 minutes.

- After that, swirl the meat and add the chili pepper and bell pepper. Continue to roast the items for around 5 minutes more.

- Mix in the tomatoes and 1/2 cup of water.

- Close the lid and simmer the food for around 10 minutes.

Nutrition Per Serving: Calories 167, Fat 9g, Carbohydrates 6g, Protein 16g, Fiber 2g, Cholesterol 46mg, Sodium 50mg, Potassium 508mg, Phosphorus 104mg

---

4. Curried Pork

Preparation time: 5 minutes | **Cooking time:** 25 minutes | **Servings:** 4

Ingredients:

- 1 cup of chopped tomatoes

- 12 oz. of pork loin, chopped

- 1 teaspoon of curry paste

- ½ teaspoon of minced ginger

- 1 tablespoon of olive oil

Instructions:

- Warm the olive oil inside a small-sized saucepan.

- After adding the chopped meat, cook for about 5 minutes. It should be stirred once in a while.

- Then, add the chopped tomatoes and minced ginger. After mixing the ingredients, cook for another 5 minutes.

- Then, add 1 1/2 cups of water and curry paste. After stirring the ingredients with a spatula till they are homogeneous, put the cover.

- Cook the beef for about 15 minutes on medium flame.

Nutrition Per Serving: Calories 253, Fat 16g, Carbohydrates 2g, Protein 24g, Fiber 1.2g, Cholesterol 68mg, Sodium 55mg, Potassium 470mg, Phosphorus 122mg

---

5. Garlic-Flavored Pork Meatballs

Preparation time: 5 minutes | **Cooking time:** 25 minutes | **Servings:** 2

Ingredients:

- 1 tablespoon of olive oil

- 2 pork medallions

- 1 teaspoon of cayenne pepper

- ¼ cup of coconut milk

- 1 teaspoon of minced garlic

Instructions:

- Each pork medallion should be seasoned using cayenne pepper and salt.

- Heat the olive oil in a skillet and add the meat.

- Roast the pork medallions for 3 minutes per side.

- Then, add the coconut milk and minced garlic. Cook for around 20 minutes on low flame with the lid closed.

Nutrition Per Serving: Calories 284, Fat 18.8g, Carbohydrates 3g, Protein 26g, Fiber 3g, Cholesterol 70mg, Sodium 60mg, Potassium 103mg, Phosphorus 53mg

---

6. Hoisin Flavored Pork

Preparation time: 10 minutes | **Cooking time:** 15 minutes | **Servings:** 4

Ingredients:

- 1 teaspoon of olive oil

- 1-pound of pork loin steaks

- Pinch of salt

- 2 tablespoons of hoisin sauce

- 1 tablespoon of apple cider vinegar

Instructions:

- Rub the pork steaks using the hoisin sauce, apple cider vinegar, salt, and olive oil.

- Preheat the grill at 395° Fahrenheit.

- Grill the pork steaks for about 7 minutes on each side.

Nutrition Per Serving: Calories 263, Fat 10g, Carbohydrates 4g, Protein 39.3g, Fiber 0.4g, Cholesterol 0mg, Sodium 130mg, Potassium 220mg, Phosphorus 92mg

7. Pork Chops in Almonds Crust

Preparation time: 5 minutes | **Cooking time:** 20 minutes | **Servings:** 4

Ingredients:

- 4 (3-4 ounces) of boneless pork chops

- 1/2 cup of grated low-fat parmesan cheese

- 1/4 cup of Dijon mustard

- 1/2 cup of almonds chopped finely

Instructions:

- Preheat the oven at 400 degrees F. Wrap foil around a baking sheet.

- Place three plates on the table. Scatter the remaining ingredients on each plate: Dijon mustard, grated parmesan, and sliced almonds.

- Apply a layer of mustard to one pork chop at a time, followed by a layer of grated cheese and chopped almonds. Spread the mixture out on a baking sheet. Preheat the oven to 350°F and add four pork chops.

- Bake for approximately 13 minutes. To avoid overcooking, check for an internal temperature of 140-145 degrees Fahrenheit. Serve with a non-starchy vegetable.

Nutrition Per Serving: Calories 287, Fat 19g, Carbohydrates 12g, Protein 28g, Fiber 1g, Cholesterol 160mg, Sodium 158mg, Potassium 399mg, Phosphorus 187mg

8. Pork Chops Curry

Preparation time: 5 minutes | **Cooking time:** 25 minutes | **Servings:** 2

Ingredients:

- 1 onion, diced

- 2 pork loin chops

- 1 tablespoon of olive oil

- ¼ cup of coconut or almond milk

- 1 teaspoon of curry powder

Instructions:

- Heat the olive oil inside a skillet.

- Cook for 5 minutes on each side of the pork chops.

- Remove the meat from the skillet and add the diced onion. Cook for 4 minutes or till the onion is soft.

- Stir in the curry powder and milk after that.

- Bring everything to a boil.

- Cook the pork chops and coat them thoroughly with the curry sauce.

- Cook for 10 minutes on low flame with the lid closed.

Nutrition Per Serving: Calories 358, Fat 27.6g, Carbohydrates 7.6g, Protein 20g, Fiber 0.4mg, Cholesterol 69mg, Sodium 74mg, Potassium 407mg, Phosphorus 87mg

9. Pork White Cabbage Rolls

Preparation time: 5 minutes | **Cooking time:** 25 minutes | **Servings:** 4

Ingredients:

- 6 oz. of lean ground pork

- ½ cup of grated carrot

- 4 white cabbage leaves

- ¼ cup of tomato puree

- 1 teaspoon of Italian seasonings

Instructions:

- Inside a mixing bowl, combine the Italian seasonings, carrot, and lean ground pork.

- Fill the white cabbage leaves with the meat mixture and place them in the tiny casserole mold to make the cabbage rolls.

- Place in a preheated 365°F oven with the tomato puree.

- Cook the cabbage rolls for about 20 minutes, then serve and enjoy.

Nutrition Per Serving: Calories 80, Fat 2g, Carbohydrates 4g, Protein 12g, Fiber 1g, Cholesterol 32mg, Sodium 41mg, Potassium 318mg, Phosphorus 100mg

10. Steak Rainbow Kebabs

Preparation time: 5 minutes | **Cooking time:** 20 minutes | **Servings:** 4

Ingredients:

- 1 small wedged onion

- 1 pound of sirloin steak

- 1/2 cup of light and low-sodium Italian dressing

- 1 cup of cherry tomatoes

- 1 peeled and sliced mango

Instructions:

- Soak wooden skewers in water for up to 30 minutes before using. To begin, preheat an outdoor grill and chop the ingredients. (Chunk the steak and combine it with the mango and onion.)

- Alter the ingredients on the skewers or combine everything on one skewer, allowing you to remove the vegetables if they're done before the meat.

- Using a large pastry brush or your hands, coat the skewers in Italian dressing.

- Grill the skewers for around 8 minutes on each side, checking frequently to ensure the vegetables are cooked to your liking.

Nutrition Per Serving: Calories 218, Fat 7g, Carbohydrates 15g, Protein 24g, Fiber 2.1g, Cholesterol 123mg, Sodium 114mg, Potassium 400mg, Phosphorus 203mg

11. Simple Beef Ranch Steak

Preparation time: 10 minutes | **Cooking time:** 15 minutes | **Servings:** 2

Ingredients:

- 1 tablespoon of olive oil

- 8 oz. of beef ranch steak

- 1 teaspoon of mustard

- Pinch of salt

- ½ teaspoon of ground nutmeg

Instructions:

- Inside a mixing bowl, combine the mustard, olive oil, salt, and ground nutmeg.

- Then smear the mustard mixture over the meat and place it on a preheated grill set at 400 degrees Fahrenheit.

- Grill the meat for approximately 8 minutes on each side.

- After that, the steaks should be sliced.

Nutrition Per Serving: Calories 465, Fat 30g, Carbohydrates 14g, Protein 23.2g, Fiber 2mg, Cholesterol 0mg, Sodium 0mg, Potassium 13mg, Phosphorus 1mg

12. Stuffed Pork with Cheese, Pesto and Spinach

Preparation time: 10 minutes | **Cooking time:** 20 minutes | **Servings:** 4

Ingredients:

- 1 cup of shredded low-fat Italian cheese blend

- 10 strips of turkey bacon

- 1 pork tenderloin (1 pound)

- 1/3 cup of prepared pesto

- 1 cup of fresh baby spinach

Instructions:

- Preheat the oven at 400 degrees F.

- Place turkey bacon strips on a chopping board, lengthwise, slightly overlapping.

- The tenderloin should be cut lengthwise along the middle and up to 1/2 inch from the bottom. Pound the tenderloin flat with a meat mallet to a thickness of 1/2 inch. Place the tenderloin in the center of the turkey bacon strips, perpendicular to the strips. Preheat the oven at 350 degrees Fahrenheit and season the pork using salt & pepper. Spread pesto on the bottom, then top with cheese and spinach. Tenderloin ends should be overlapping with turkey bacon. Tie at 3-inch intervals with kitchen cord. To keep the ends together, toothpicks are used.

- Bake for about 20 minutes, rotating halfway.

Nutrition Per Serving: Calories 402, Fat 25g, Carbohydrates 4g, Protein 37g, Fiber 1.2g, Cholesterol 205.3mg, Sodium 246mg, Potassium 547.5mg, Phosphorus 261mg

13. Spiced Beef

Preparation time: 5 minutes | **Cooking time:** 25 minutes | **Servings:** 4

Ingredients:

- 1-pound of beef sirloin

- 1 teaspoon of peppercorn

- 2 cups of water

- 1 bay leaf

- 1 tablespoon of five-spice seasoning

Instructions:

- Season the meat in an instant pot with five-spice seasoning.

- Pour in the bay leaf, 1 1/2 cups of water, and peppercorns.

- Cook for around 20 minutes on High heat with the lid closed.

- Pour the hot spiced water from the pot over the cooked meat and serve.

Nutrition Per Serving: Calories 213, Fat 7g, Carbohydrates 1g, Protein 34.5g, Fiber 2g, Cholesterol 101mg, Sodium 116mg, Potassium 466mg, Phosphorus 132mg

14. Southwestern-Style Steak

Preparation time: 10 minutes | **Cooking time:** 15 minutes | **Servings:** 2

Ingredients:

- 1 tablespoon of lemon juice

- 1 teaspoon of garlic powder

- 2 beef flank steaks

- 1 tablespoon of avocado oil

- 1 teaspoon of chili flakes

Instructions:

- Preheat the grill at 385° Fahrenheit.

- The beef should then be seasoned using garlic powder, salt and chili flakes.

- Then drizzle with avocado oil and lemon juice to finish.

- On a hot grill, grill the steaks for about 8 minutes on each side.

Nutrition Per Serving: Calories 174, Fat 6.3g, Carbohydrates 2g, Protein 26.2g, Fiber 1g, Cholesterol 76mg, Sodium 58mg, Potassium 392mg, Phosphorus 171mg

15. Tender Pork Medallions

Preparation time: 5 minutes | **Cooking time:** 25 minutes | **Servings:** 3

Ingredients:

- ½ cup of low-fat yogurt

- 1 teaspoon of dried sage

- 12 oz. of pork tenderloin

- 1 tablespoon of margarine

- 1 teaspoon of ground black pepper

Instructions:

- Season the pork tenderloin in three medallions with salt, sage and black pepper.

- Melt the margarine in a saucepan and add the pork medallions.

- Cook for about 5 minutes per side.

- Then add the yogurt and coat the meat thoroughly.

- Close the lid and cook the medallions for about 15 minutes on medium flame.

Nutrition Per Serving: Calories 227, Fat 8.3g, Carbohydrates 4g, Protein 32.4g, Fiber 0.4mg, Cholesterol 85mg, Sodium 138mg, Potassium 586mg, Phosphorus 217mg

Chapter 11: Desserts and Treats

1. Apple Nachos Dessert

Preparation time: 10 minutes | **Cooking time:** 0 minute | **Servings:** 6

Ingredients:

- ½ cup of sugar-free caramel sauce

- 2 oz. of melted dark chocolate

- 1/4 cup of chopped peanuts

- 4 Granny Smith apples

- 1/4 cup of melted peanut butter

Instructions:

- Apples must be peeled and sliced thinly. Arrange apples on a baking sheet or a pan.

- Over the apples, drizzle with melted peanut butter, caramel sauce, and dark chocolate.

- Sprinkle with chopped nuts before serving.

Nutrition Per Serving: Calories 142, Total Fat 6g, Protein 3g, Carbs 23g, Fiber 0g, Cholesterol 13mg, Sodium 233mg, Potassium 55mg, Phosphorus 4mg

2. Avocado Mousse

Preparation time: 10 minutes | **Cooking time:** 0 minutes | **Servings:** 2

Ingredients:

- 1 teaspoon of vanilla extract

- ½ cup of low-fat milk

- 1 avocado, peeled and pitted

- 1 tablespoon of cocoa powder

- 2 teaspoons of liquid honey

Instructions:

- Put the avocado inside a food processor and blitz it.

- Add the milk, vanilla extract, and cocoa powder.

- Blend till the mixture is completely smooth.

- Pour cooked mousse halfway into the glasses and drizzle with honey.

Nutrition Per Serving: Calories 264, Fat 20g, Carbohydrates 18g, Protein 4.5g, Fiber 1mg, Cholesterol 3mg, Sodium 34mg, Potassium 653mg, Phosphorus 183mg

3. Coconut Mousse

Preparation time: 5 minutes | **Cooking time:** 15 minutes | **Servings:** 4

Ingredients:

- 3 cups of low-fat milk

- 3 tablespoons of liquid honey

- 2 tablespoons of coconut flakes

- 3 tablespoons of corn starch

Instructions:

- Bring the milk to boil before stirring in the cornstarch and coconut flakes.

- Cook the mousse for 2 minutes on low flame.

- Allow the dessert to cool before adding the honey liquid.

Nutrition Per Serving: Calories 53, Fat 1g, Carbohydrates 10g, Protein 2g, Fiber 0.1mg, Cholesterol 3mg, Sodium 27mg, Potassium 97mg, Phosphorus 28mg

4. Choco Frosty

Preparation time: 15 minutes | **Cooking time:** 0 minutes | **Servings:** 2

Ingredients:

- 1 cup of heavy cream
- 1 teaspoon of vanilla
- 8 drops of liquid stevia
- 1 tablespoon of almond butter
- 2 tablespoons of unsweetened cocoa powder

Instructions:

- Combine all of the ingredients in a mixing bowl. Beat with an immersion blender till soft peaks form.
- Place in the refrigerator for about 30 minutes.
- Fill the piping bag halfway with the icy mixture and pipe it into the serving glasses.
- After serving, relax and enjoy.

Nutrition Per Serving: Calories 240, Total Fat 25g, Protein 3g, Carbs 4g, Fiber 2g, Cholesterol 15mg, Sodium 150mg, Potassium 310mg, Phosphorus 72mg

5. Cardamom Black Rice Pudding

Preparation time: 10 minutes | **Cooking time:** 20 minutes | **Servings:** 4

Ingredients:

- ½ cup of natural sweetener
- 2 cups of wild rice
- 1 teaspoon of ground cardamom
- 5 cups of water

Instructions:

- Combine rice, water, and ground cinnamon together in a pot.

- Cook the rice for around 20 minutes on low flame.

- Stir in the natural sweetener till everything is well combined.

Nutrition Per Serving: Calories 413, Fat 2g, Carbohydrates 45g, Protein 2g, Fiber 0.2g, Cholesterol 0mg, Sodium 43mg, Potassium 375mg, Phosphorus 72mg

6. Dark Chocolate Strawberries

Preparation time: 10 minutes | **Cooking time:** 2 minutes | **Servings:** 2

Ingredients:

- 1 cup of strawberries

- 2 tablespoons of chopped dark chocolate

- 1 tablespoon of olive oil

Instructions:

- Melt the chocolate in the microwave for 10 seconds. If 10 seconds is insufficient, repeat the process for another 10 seconds.

- Then, in a mixing bowl, combine the chocolate and olive oil. Everything should be thoroughly combined.

- Freeze the strawberries for 10 minutes in the freezer.

- Coat them with the chocolate mixture using a pastry brush.

Nutrition Per Serving: Calories 159, Fat 12g, Carbohydrates 14g, Protein 2g, Fiber 1g, Cholesterol 3mg, Sodium 12mg, Potassium 163mg, Phosphorus 11mg

7. Fruit Kebabs

Preparation time: 10 minutes | **Cooking time:** 0 minutes | **Servings:** 3

Ingredients:

- 1 cup of cubed melon

- 1 cup of cubed watermelon

- 2 cubed kiwis

- 1 cup of strawberries

- 1 cup of grapes

Instructions:

- Thread the fruits onto the wooden skewers one at a time.

- Fruit kebabs should be refrigerated for no more than 30 minutes.

Nutrition Per Serving: Calories 100, Fat 1g, Carbohydrates 19g, Protein 2g, Fiber 0.2mg, Cholesterol 0mg, Sodium 12mg, Potassium 485mg, Phosphorus 100mg

---

8. Lemon-Blackberry Frozen Yogurt

Preparation time: 15 minutes | **Cooking time:** 0 minutes | **Servings:** 2

Ingredients:

- 1/4 cup of low-fat plain Greek yogurt

- 1 teaspoon of liquid stevia

- Juice of 1 lemon

- 2 cups of frozen blackberries

- Fresh mint leaves, for garnish

Instructions:

- Inside a blender or food processor, combine the blackberries, lemon juice, yogurt, and stevia. Blend for about five minutes, or till smooth.

- After serving, relax and enjoy.

Nutrition Per Serving: Calories 68, Total Fat 0g, Protein 3g, Carbs 15g, Fiber 0g, Cholesterol 0mg, Sodium 90mg, Potassium 301mg, Phosphorus 81mg

9. Milky Fudge

Preparation time: 5 minutes | **Cooking time:** 10 minutes | **Servings:** 4

Ingredients:

- ½ cup of cocoa powder
- 1 cup of low-fat milk
- ½ cup of margarine
- 1 teaspoon of vanilla extract

Instructions:

- Heat the milk inside a saucepan over medium flame, then whisk in the margarine and cook for about 7 minutes.
- Take the pan off the flame and stir in the cocoa powder.
- Fill a lined square pan halfway with the mixture, flatten it, and place it in the refrigerator for 1 to 2 hours.

Nutrition Per Serving: Calories 85, Fat 8g, Carbohydrates 3g, Protein 2g, Fiber 0.2mg, Cholesterol 1mg, Sodium 98mg, Potassium 125mg, Phosphorus 43mg

10. Protein Cinnamon Roll Dip

Preparation time: 10 minutes | **Cooking time:** 0 minute | **Servings:** 5

Ingredients:

- 8 oz. of Greek yogurt cream cheese
- 1/4 cup of almond milk
- 2 scoops of vanilla protein powder
- 4 oz. of Greek yogurt
- 1 teaspoon of cinnamon

Instructions:

- Allow the cream cheese to come to room temperature before using it.
- Using a mixer, thoroughly combine all of the ingredients.

- Before serving, sprinkle cinnamon on top.

- Serve with your favorite cookie substitutes, apples, or other fruit as a side dish.

Nutrition Per Serving: Calories 109, Total Fat 5g, Protein 10g, Carbs 6g, Fiber 2g, Cholesterol 10mg, Sodium 240mg, Potassium 124mg, Phosphorus 12mg

---

11. Peanut Butter Fluff

Preparation time: 5 minutes | **Cooking time:** 0 minute | **Servings:** 2

Ingredients:

- 1 scoop of vanilla protein powder

- 3 tablespoons of natural peanut butter

- 1/2 teaspoon of vanilla extract

- 1 packet of Splenda

- 6 oz. of Greek yogurt

Instructions:

- Mix all of the ingredients thoroughly using a hand mixer. Choose your favorite toppings!

Nutrition Per Serving: Calories 287, Total Fat 13g, Protein 26g, Carbs 15g, Fiber 7g, Cholesterol 0mg, Sodium 210mg, Potassium 100mg, Phosphorus 11mg

12. Peanut Butter Cookies

Preparation time: 10 minutes | **Cooking time:** 15 minutes | **Servings:** 2

Ingredients:

- Nonstick cooking spray
- 1/4 cup of stevia baking blend
- 1/2 cup of natural smooth peanut butter
- 1/2 large egg
- 1/4 teaspoon of vanilla extract

Instructions:

- Preheat oven at 350°F. Coat a nonstick baking sheet using parchment paper or cooking spray.
- Inside a medium-sized mixing bowl, combine the peanut butter, stevia, egg, and vanilla extract with a hand mixer.
- After rolling the batter into 1-inch balls, place them on the baking sheet. Flatten each ball to about 1/4-inch thickness. Using a fork, make two crisscrossing imprints on the cookie.
- Bake for approximately 12 minutes. The cookies are done when they are golden brown.

- After 5 minutes, transfer to a cooling rack to finish the process.

Nutrition Per Serving: Calories 107, Total Fat 9g, Protein 4g, Carbs 4g, Fiber 0.8g, Cholesterol 21mg, Sodium 128mg, Potassium 66mg, Phosphorus 13mg

13. Protein Fudgecicles

Preparation time: 10 minutes | **Cooking time:** 0 minute | **Servings:** 4

Ingredients:

- 2 scoops of chocolate protein powder

- 4 oz. of almond milk

- 1 cup of cool light whip

Instructions:

- Inside a protein shaker, combine the cocoa, milk, and protein powder.

- Last, fold in the cold whip.

- Fill popsicle molds halfway with the mixture and freeze for at least an hour or till set.

Nutrition Per Serving: Calories 85, Total Fat 3g, Protein 7g, Carbs 9g, Fiber 0.5mg, Cholesterol 4.4mg, Sodium 89mg, Potassium 70mg, Phosphorus 26mg

14. Sugar-Free Banana Cookies

Preparation time: 5 minutes | **Cooking time:** 20 minutes | **Servings:** 13 cookies

Ingredients:

- 1/2 teaspoon of baking powder

- 2 ripe bananas

- 1/3 cup of almond milk

- 1 cup of almond flour

Instructions:

- Preheat the oven at 350°F.

- Peel and mash the bananas inside a mixing bowl. Stir in the almond milk till everything is well combined.

- Stir in the flour and baking powder till the mixture is smooth and thick.

- Place 13 equal-sized blobs of batter on a baking sheet lined using parchment paper using an ice cream scoop.

- Bake the cookies for approximately 10-15 minutes.

- Allow them to cool slightly before serving.

Nutrition Per Serving: Calories 52, Total Fat 0.1g, Protein 1g, Carbs 11g, Fiber 1g, Cholesterol 15mg, Sodium 125mg, Potassium 0mg, Phosphorus 0mg

15. Three Ingredients Cookie

Preparation time: 5 minutes | **Cooking time:** 20 minutes | **Servings:** 16

Ingredients:

- 1/2 cup of mini dark chocolate chips

- Dash of salt

- 1 cup of quick-cooking oats

- 2 ripe bananas

Instructions:

- Mash your bananas thoroughly.

- Combine the oats and chocolate.

- Season with salt.

- Stir till all of the ingredients are covered and well combined.

- Drop spoonfuls of dough (16 cookies) onto a cookie sheet and slightly flatten them to make cookies.

- Preheat the oven at 350°F and bake for about 15 minutes.

Nutrition Per Serving: Calories 86, Total Fat 3g, Protein 2g, Carbs 14g, Fiber 1g, Cholesterol 16mg, Sodium 161mg, Potassium 42mg, Phosphorus 12mg

Chapter 12: Dressing, Sauces and Seasonings Recipes

1. Asian-Style Stir Fry Sauce

Preparation time: 5 minutes | **Cooking time:** 0 minute | **Servings:** 6

Ingredients:

- 1 teaspoon of onion powder

- 2 teaspoons of sesame oil

- 1 teaspoon of dried minced garlic

- 1/2 cup of coconut aminos

- 1 teaspoon of ginger powder

Instructions:

- Inside a small-sized mixing bowl, combine all of the ingredients. Place the mixture in an airtight container and place it in the refrigerator. Stir-fries and sautés are great ways to use them.

Nutrition Per Serving: Calories 32, Total Fat 2g, Protein 0.1g, Carbs 2g, Fiber 0g, Cholesterol 0.2mg, Sodium 161mg, Potassium 23mg, Phosphorus 2mg

2. Cajun Seasoning Mix

Preparation time: 5 minutes | **Cooking time:** 0 minutes | **Servings:** 4

Ingredients:

- 1 tablespoon of paprika

- 1 tablespoon of dried oregano

- ½ tablespoon of salt

- 1 tablespoon of ground black pepper

- 1 tablespoon of cayenne pepper

Instructions:

- In a plastic bag, combine the oregano, cayenne pepper, salt, paprika, and black pepper.

Nutrition Per Serving: Calories 3, Fat 0.1g, Carbohydrates 1g, Protein 0.1g, Fiber 0mg, Cholesterol 0mg, Sodium 4mg, Potassium 21.4mg, Phosphorus 4.3mg

3. Homemade Lemon Vinaigrette

Preparation time: 5 minutes | **Cooking time:** 0 minute | **Servings:** 1/2 cup

Ingredients:

- 6 tablespoons of extra virgin olive oil

- 1/8 teaspoon of coarsely ground pepper

- 2 teaspoons of Dijon mustard

- 2 tablespoons of fresh lemon juice

- 1/4 teaspoon of salt

Instructions:

- Using a whisk, combine everything except the olive oil in a large mixing bowl. Pour in the olive oil slowly, stirring constantly.

Nutrition Per Serving: Calories 183, Total Fat 20g, Protein 0g, Carbs 1g, Fiber 0.3g, Cholesterol 0mg, Sodium 251mg, Potassium 18mg, Phosphorus 0.4mg

4. Hollandaise Sauce

Preparation time: 5 minutes | **Cooking time**: 0 minute | **Servings**: 4

Ingredients:

- 7 oz. of butter

- 1 tablespoon of lemon juice

- 1 egg

- Salt to taste

Instructions:

- In a mixing bowl, crack an egg.

- Melt the butter in a pourable container that can be microwaved or heated on the stovetop.

- While holding an immersion blender in one hand, slowly pour the melted butter into the egg bowl. The bottom layer should turn white and creamy before you move the blender to the next layer. It's done when the sauce is thick and airy.

- Stir in the lemon juice and season using salt to taste.

Nutrition Per Serving: Calories 78, Total Fat 42g, Protein 2g, Carbs 0.4g, Fiber 0.3g, Cholesterol 33mg, Sodium 518mg, Potassium 27mg, Phosphorus 2.4mg

5. Homemade Dill Dressing

Preparation time: 5 minutes | **Cooking time**: 0 minute | **Servings**: 2 cups

Ingredients:

- 3 sprigs of fresh dill

- 2 cups of roughly chopped dill pickles

- 1/4 cup of dill pickle juice

- Salt and black pepper to taste

- 1/4 cup of canola oil

Instructions:

- In a blender, combine the dill pickles, fresh dill, pickle juice, olive oil, salt, and pepper till smooth.

Nutrition Per Serving: Calories 17, Total Fat 1.8g, Protein 0.1g, Carbs 0.4g, Fiber 0.1g, Cholesterol 13mg, Sodium 109mg, Potassium 60mg, Phosphorus 11mg

6. Homemade Lemon Tahini Dressing

Preparation time: 10 minutes | **Cooking time:** 0 minute | **Servings:** 16

Ingredients:

- 6 cloves of pressed garlic cloves

- 8 tablespoons of tahini

- 1 tablespoon of coarse salt

- 1/2 cup of olive oil

- 1 cup of lemon juice

Instructions:

- In a container with a lid, combine the olive oil, lemon juice, and tahini. Shake the jar vigorously till everything is thoroughly combined. Using a garlic press, mash the garlic into the dressing. Shake vigorously and sprinkle with salt.

Nutrition Per Serving: Calories 110, Total Fat 10.8g, Protein 1.4g, Carbs 3.3, Fiber 0.5g, Cholesterol 0mg, Sodium 38mg, Potassium 57mg, Phosphorus 28mg

7. Low-Carb White Sauce

Preparation time: 5 minutes | **Cooking time:** 10 minutes | **Servings:** 4

Ingredients:

- 1 egg yolk

- 1/2 cup (4 oz.) of cream cheese

- Salt and pepper, to taste

- 1/2 cup of heavy cream

- 1/4 cup of water

Instructions:

- Inside a saucepan, combine the cream cheese, cream, and water and heat over low flame till the cream cheese melts.

- To temper the egg yolk, whisk a small amount of the cream sauce into it, then return it to the cream sauce.

- Stir the sauce frequently over a low flame for a few minutes, or till it thickens.

- Season using salt and pepper to taste.

Nutrition Per Serving: Calories 214, Total Fat 21g, Protein 3g, Carbs 2.2g, Fiber 0.1g, Cholesterol 19mg, Sodium 63mg, Potassium 75mg, Phosphorus 21mg

8. Lemon-Pepper Seasoning Mix

Preparation time: 5 minutes | **Cooking time:** 25 minutes | **Servings:** 4

Ingredients:

- 2 tablespoons of multi-colored peppercorns

- ¼ teaspoon of dehydrated onion flakes

- 2 lemons

- Pinch of salt

- ¼ teaspoon of dehydrated minced garlic

Instructions:

- Preheat oven at 200°F. Line a baking sheet using parchment paper.

- Lemons should be washed and dried before use. Remove the zest from both lemons using a vegetable peeler, being careful not to get any of the pith. Arrange the peels in a single layer on the lined baking sheet.

- Bake for around 20 minutes in a preheated oven or until the peels have curled and dried. Allow the lemon peels to cool for about 20 minutes inside the turned-off oven, propped open with a wooden spoon to allow moisture to escape. Remove the pan from the oven and allow it to cool completely before proceeding to the next step.

- Combine dried lemon peels, peppercorns, and salt in a food processor fitted with a blade. Blend till the mixture is coarse. Dry the onion and garlic and add them. Blend till smooth and well combined.

Nutrition Per Serving: Calories 11, Fat 0.2g, Carbohydrates 4g, Protein 0.4g, Fiber 0.1mg, Cholesterol 0mg, Sodium 2.1mg, Potassium 42.5mg, Phosphorus 11mg

9. Russian-Style Salad Dressing

Preparation time: 5 minutes | **Cooking time:** 0 minute | **Servings:** 8

Ingredients:

- 1 tablespoon of red wine vinegar
- 1/2 cup of low-fat mayonnaise
- 1 tablespoon of finely chopped onion
- 1/3 cup of ketchup
- Salt and pepper to taste

Instructions:

- Mix the mayonnaise, salt, ketchup, vinegar, onion, and pepper in a small bowl till well combined. Keep it in the fridge till you're ready to use it.

Nutrition Per Serving: Calories 110, Total Fat 10.9g, Protein 0.3g, Carbs 3.2g, Fiber 0g, Cholesterol 8mg, Sodium 270mg, Potassium 19mg, Phosphorus 2mg

10. Za'atar Spice

Preparation time: 5 minutes | **Cooking time:** 3 minutes | **Servings:** 4

Ingredients:

- 3 tablespoons of sesame seeds
- 3 tablespoons of fresh thyme leaves
- 1 tablespoon of sumac powder
- ½ tablespoon of salt

Instructions:

- Toast sesame seeds in a dry skillet over medium flame for 3 to 5 minutes or till golden brown.
- In a mixing bowl, combine sesame seeds, salt, thyme leaves, and sumac till well combined.

Nutrition Per Serving: Calories 29, Fat 2g, Carbohydrates 2g, Protein 1g, Fiber 0mg, Cholesterol 0mg, Sodium 19mg, Potassium 40mg, Phosphorus 11mg

Measurement Conversion Table

CUP	OUNCES	MILLILITERS	TABLESPOONS
8 cup	64 oz.	1895 ml	128
6 cup	48 oz.	1420 ml	96
5 cup	40 oz.	1180 ml	80
4 cup	32 oz.	960 ml	64
2 cup	16 oz.	480 ml	32
1 cup	8 oz.	240 ml	16
3/4 cup	6 oz.	177 ml	12
2/3 cup	5 oz.	158 ml	11
1/2 cup	4 oz.	118 ml	8
3/8 cup	3 oz.	90 ml	6
1/3 cup	2.5 oz.	79 ml	5.5
1/4 cup	2 oz.	59 ml	4
1/8 cup	1 oz.	30 ml	3
1/16 cup	1/2 oz.	15 ml	1

Conclusion

Thank you for reading all the way through Bariatric Cookbook Bible. We hope it was informative and provided you with all of the tools you need to achieve your goals, whatever they may be.

A bariatric surgery alters the way food enters your intestines by reducing the size of your stomach. Following the procedure, getting enough nutrition while losing weight is critical.

If you believe bariatric surgery is right for you, the next step is to consult with your doctor. If you've already had the surgery, start experimenting with these recipes. Finally, if you have surgery coming up, there are plenty of recipes to help you get through it. Good luck!

Resources

Academy of Nutrition & Dietetics

www.eatright.org

You can find a wealth of knowledge about nutrition and health at the Academy of Nutrition & Dietetics' website.

It boasts membership from every continent except Antarctica, and is the world's largest association of nutrition and food experts.

American Society for the Metabolic & the Bariatric Surgery

www.asmbs.org

When it comes to bariatric surgery and the treatment of obesity, nobody does more than the ASMBS, the American Society for Metabolic & the Bariatric Surgery.

Baritastic and MyFitnessPal

www.baritastic.com and www.myfitnesspal.com

The results of studies show that dieters who keep food diaries have a better success rate at losing weight. You can set reminders, research the nutritional value of foods, determine the nutritional value of recipes, and more with free exercise and food trackers like Baritastic and MyFitnessPal.

BariatricPal

www.bariatricpal.com

People who have had bariatric surgery can find support from others who have gone through the same thing on this website. You will also be able to read reviews of local surgeons and learn more generally about surgery.

Obesity Action Coalition

www.obesityaction.org

A group working on a national level to help those who suffer from obesity. You can find informational materials, assistance programs, and chances to network with other members of the OAC community on their website.

ObesityHelp

www.obesityhelp.com

ObesityHelp is a forum for those involved in the field of bariatrics, including doctors, patients, and loved ones. People who have had or are considering having weight-loss surgery will find helpful discussion boards, guides, and recipes here.

The Obesity Society

www.obesity.org

TOS (The Obesity Society) is an academic organization concerned with the study, management, and prevention of obesity. You can find out more about their annual gathering, ObesityWeek, & their journal, Obesity, which publishes the most recent findings in the treatment of obesity by visiting their website.

References

- Academy of Nutrition & Dietetics. "Bariatric Surgery." *Nutrition Care Manual.* Accessed July 5, 2019.
  http://www.nutritioncaremanual.org.

- Linda Aills and others. "ASMBS Allied Health Nutrient Guidelines for Patients Undergoing Surgical Weight Loss." *Surgery for Obesity & Related Illnesses* 4, no. 5 (2008) doi:10.1016/j.soard.2008.03.002.

- Cummings, A. Isom, Kellene, and Sue. *Academy of Nutrition & Dietetics Pocket Guide to the Bariatric Surgery.* Academy of Nutrition and Dietetics, year 2015.

- Shiri Sherf, Dagan, and others. "Nutritional Suggestions for the Adult

- "Clinical Practice Principles for the Nutritional, Metabolic, & Nonsurgical Support of the Bariatric Surgery Patient"— Update of 2013: Cosponsored by the American Association of Clinical Endocrinologists, The American Society for Metabolic & Bariatric Surgery & the Obesity Society," Jeffrey Mechanick and others. *Endocrine Practice* 19, no. 2 (2013): 337–372., doi:10.4158/ep12437.gl.

- Julie, jarrott, and others. "American Society for the Metabolic & the Bariatric Surgery Integrated Health Nutritional principles for the Weight Loss Surgical Patient year 2016 Update: Micronutrients." *Surgery for the Obesity & the Related Illnesses* 13, no. 5 (2017): 727–741., doi:10.1016/j.soard.2016.12.018.

Dear Valued Customers,

I am thrilled to present you with an exclusive opportunity to enhance your cooking experience with my cookbook! As a token of our appreciation for your support, I invite you to download a complimentary PDF containing all the mouthwatering images of our recipes. Simply scan the QR code below to access this delightful addition to your culinary journey.

🔍 Four Reasons to Download the PDF:

Enhanced Visual Experience: By accessing the PDF, you'll enjoy high-quality images of each recipe, showcasing the vibrant colors, textures, and presentation details that truly bring our dishes to life. With crisp, detailed visuals at your fingertips, you can better visualize your culinary creations and inspire your cooking adventures.

Convenience and Accessibility: Unlike traditional cookbooks, where space constraints may limit the number of images included, our separate PDF ensures that you have access to every recipe's visual representation. Whether you're planning your next meal at home or browsing for inspiration on the go, having a digital copy of the images provides unparalleled convenience and accessibility.

Cost Efficiency: Printing high-quality images directly in the cookbook significantly increases production costs, which ultimately leads to higher purchasing prices for our customers. By offering a separate PDF for the recipe images, we can maintain an affordable price point for the cookbook while still providing you with stunning visuals to complement your cooking experience.

Personalization and Sharing: The PDF format empowers you to personalize your cooking experience. Easily print out your favorite recipe images for your kitchen inspiration board or see it in your tablet or mobile while cooking. With the ability to save, print, and share the images, you can spread the joy of cooking and create lasting memories with loved ones.

▦ Scan the QR Code Below to Get Started:

Thank you for choosing my cookbook to accompany you on your culinary adventures. I hope this additional resource enriches your cooking journey and inspires countless delicious meals in your kitchen.

Enjoyed Our Cookbook? Leave a Review on Amazon! If you've enjoyed my cookbook and the complimentary gift of recipe images, I would greatly appreciate it if you could take a moment to leave a positive review on Amazon. Your feedback helps me continue to provide excellent resources and inspires others to discover the joy of cooking with my recipes.

Happy cooking!

Alex Mc Corner